# Contents

American Batsford Chess Library

# A Complete Defense for Black

Raymond Keene and Byron Jacobs

An ICE Book
International Chess Enterprises, Seattle

International Chess Enterprises, Inc.
2005 Fifth Avenue, Suite 402
Seattle, Washington 98121-2850

P. O. Box 19457
Seattle, Washington 98109-1457

First published 1996

Typeset by B. B. Enterprises, Brighton and printed in Great Britain by Redwood Books, Trowbridge, Wilts, for the publishers, B. T. Batsford Ltd, 4 Fitzhardinge Street, London W1H 0AH

First published in the United States in 1996 by
International Chess Enterprises, Inc.
Originally published in Great Britain in 1996 by
B. T. Batsford Ltd.

*To the memory and achievements of the Russian grandmaster Efim Bogoljubow*

ISBN 1-879479-34-6 (An ICE Book: pbk.)

First American Edition - 1996

Printed in the United Kingdom
All first editions are printed on acid-free paper.

*Editorial Panel:* Mark Dvoretsky, Jon Speelman
*General Adviser:* Raymond Keene OBE
*Specialist Adviser:* Dr John Nunn
*Commissioning Editor:* Graham Burgess

# Bibliography

*ChessBase Magazine 1-52*, ChessBase GmbH
*Informator 1-64*, Sahovski Informator
Keene and Jacobs, *An Opening Repertoire for the Attacking Player*,
Batsford 1995
Matanovic, *Encyclopaedia of Chess Openings, Volume C*, Sahovski
Informator 1981
Matanovic, *Encyclopaedia of Chess Openings, Volume D*, Sahovski
Informator 1987
Nimzowitsch, *My System,* Batsford
Nimzowitsch, *Chess Praxis,* Batsford
Reti, *Masters of the Chessboard,* Batsford
Keene and Schiller, *Winning with the Hypermodern,* Batsford 1994
Keene, *Aron Nimzowitsch, Master of Strategy,* Batsford
Kasparov and Keene, *Batsford Chess Openings 2,* Batsford 1988
Gufeld, *An Opening Repertoire for the Attacking Player,* Cadogan
1996
Charushin, *A Single Passion - but an Ardent One,* Victor Charushin
1995

# Symbols

| | |
|---|---|
| + | Check |
| ++ | Double check |
| ! | Good move |
| !! | Excellent move |
| ? | Bad move |
| ?? | Blunder |
| !? | Interesting move |
| ?! | Dubious move |
| OL | Olympiad |
| Ch. | Championship |
| Z | Zonal |
| IZ | Interzonal |
| 1-0 | Black resigns |
| ½-½ | Draw agreed |
| 0-1 | White resigns |

# Foreword

How often have you stared at the acres and acres of books, articles and computer disks devoted to the ever-expanding mass of openings theory - and despaired? It seems that as we know more and more about chess, instead of shrinking the possibilities and pruning away variations that do not work, the universe of chess theory continues to grow as if fuelled by a cosmic Big Bang.

Surely, at some point, you must have wished that as Black you could choose just one single opening move against any White system and be confident that there was a method applicable to all openings to back this up. In the early 1970s Ray Keene (here a co-author) sought to do this with his book *The Modern Defence*. Then the suggestion was for Black to play 1...g6 and 2...♗g7 more or less irrespective of White's opening moves. At the time, it seemed a universal panacea. Now, even the Modern Defence has exploded into a massive complex of super-highways and spaghetti junctions. Its ramifications go far beyond the immediate grasp of the enthusiastic amateur or club and county player.

What we have tried to do in this book is to provide a modern defence for the 1990s and the 21st century. We advocate the surprising move 1...♘c6 as the answer to every White opening! What are the advantages of this? First of all, the lines are unusual, so the White player will be thrown immediately upon his or her own resources. Secondly, 1...♘c6 is a pleasant blend of soundness and aggression. There are few Black defences in which White can be overrun with such devastating rapidity, as numerous Black wins in this book will testify. Finally, this defence enjoys the sanction of many top champions and grandmasters. Lines with ...♘c6 have been favourites with ex-world champion Vassily Smyslov, also with the two-times world championship challengers, Mikhail Chigorin and Efim Bogoljubow. Hard hitting British grandmaster Tony Miles has elevated 1...♘c6 to one of his main defences, while even such a classically minded player as Nigel Short, Britain's own world championship challenger, has utilised versions of the ...♘c6 defence in his own games.

By playing ...♘c6 on move one, Black is able to play across many White systems and thus avoid the most dangerous lines. For example after 1 d4 ♘c6 2 c4 we recommend 2...e5, while against 1 d4 ♘c6 2 ♘f3 we now counsel transposition to the Chigorin Defence where White has forfeited the option of a very early ♘c3 (i.e. 1 d4 ♘c6 2 c4 d5 3 ♘c3!) which makes this line risky for Black in the main variations. Similarly, after 1 e4 ♘c6 2 d4, Black is by no means committed to 2...d5 when once again there can follow 3 ♘c3! which renders this line equally risky for the second player. We prefer 1 e4 ♘c6 2 d4 e5, which is sound, reliable and full of counter-chances.

In conclusion, we would like to draw particular attention to the section in this book which starts 1 d4 ♘c6 2 d5 in which White takes up the challenge of playing a mirror image to Alekhine's Defence (1 e4 ♘f6 2 e5) on the other side of the board. This has been championed especially by Bogoljubow and Miles, who have notched up excellent results with it. Alekhine's Defence has been popular since the 1920s, yet this parallel line, which we name Bogoljubow's Defence, has, in comparison, been unjustly neglected. We regard it as fully the equal of Alekhine's Defence and invite you, the readers, to join us at what might be termed the theoretical birth of a fascinating and hitherto under-analysed line which we hope will score heavily for you in your own games as Black.

Raymond Keene and Byron Jacobs,
London,
July 1996

# 1 Introduction to 1...♞c6: Strategic Themes and History

In this book we recommend an unusual but sound defence. This is based on the immediate development of Black's queen's knight against both kingside, queenside and even fianchetto openings. It has been patronised by Nigel Short, Jon Speelman and, particularly, Tony Miles, while in the past it has numbered such greats as Mikhail Chigorin, Aron Nimzowitsch and Efim Bogoljubow amongst its devotees. It has even been played by former world champion Smyslov against Garry Kasparov, a game where, after a fluctuating struggle, Smyslov held the draw (see page 38 for the full game).

A chief merit of the queen's knight's defence is that it immediately throws booked-up white players onto their own resources with the result that Black can often score quick and crushing knockouts, as many games from this introduction will show. A further, practical, benefit for Black players is that many players, when confronted with an unusual variation, will spend a great deal of time in the early stages of the game, thus leaving themselves short of time for the more critical positions later on.

## Section A
## Against the d-pawn

Game 1
**Kaidanov-Miles**
*Palma 1989*

1    d4        ♞c6

This is the essential move of Black's defence, whatever first move White chooses. In this specific line, Black challenges White to start an immediate hunt of the black queen's knight, with 2 d5, which can lead to thrilling tactics and combinations.

**2 e4**

White refuses the invitation to join the hunt.

**2 ... e5**

This is the move we mainly recommend in the book, though Nimzowitsch's favourite 2...d5 is certainly playable and examples of it will figure later in this introduction.

**3 d5**

Now this space-gaining thrust gives Black's defence its specific character. White could, of course, play 3 ♞f3 transposing to the Scotch Game (see games 23 and 24).

**3 ... ♞ce7**

**4 c4**

Although White has played 2 e4, this move marks this variation out as a queenside opening.

**4 ... ♞g6**

**5 ♝e3 ♝b4+**

By developing the king's bishop in this fashion Black aims to weaken White on the dark squares. In particular the manoeuvre ...♝b4, followed by ...♝a5 and ...♝b6, has been known since the 19th century. One example was 1 e4 ♞c6 2 d4 e5 3 d5 ♞ce7 4 ♞f3 ♞g6 5 ♝e3 ♝b4+ 6 c3 ♝a5 7 ♝d3 ♝b6, Williams-Kennedy, London 1848.

**6 ♞d2 ♞f6**

**7 f3 ♛e7**

**8 g3**

White wants to keep Black's knight out of f4. However, the desire to restrict the activity of Black's pieces on the kingside frequently leads to White's pawn structure becoming over-extended and unwieldy.

**8 ... 0-0**

**9 ♝h3?! c6!**

Preparing to set the board alight with tactical complications. The simple 9...d6, offering exchanges, would be quite satisfactory, but perhaps a little too stereotyped.

**10 a3 ♝c5**

**11 ♞f1 b5!**

Black has a clear initiative.

**12 b4 ♝d4!**

Offering a pawn, if only temporarily, to blast open the board whilst White's men are still asleep in their beds.

| 13 | ♗xd4 | exd4 |
|----|------|------|
| 14 | ♕xd4 |      |

Black was threatening to play ...♘xe4 with devastation.

| 14 | ... | bxc4 |
|----|-----|------|
| 15 | d6  |      |

White can scarcely hope to survive after 15 dxc6 d5. The text tries to seal things up.

| 15 | ...  | ♕e5 |
|----|------|-----|
| 16 | ♘e2  | a5  |

Black, in contrast, is anxious to open as many lines as possible as quickly as possible, before White can consolidate his position.

| 17 | ♘e3  | axb4 |
|----|------|------|
| 18 | ♘xc4 | ♕h5  |
| 19 | ♗g2  | c5!  |
| 20 | ♕e3  | ♗a6  |

With the entry of Black's bishop at long last into the game, Black's advantage is finally clear.

| 21 | ♘b6 | ♖ab8 |
|----|-----|------|

| 22 | axb4 |
|----|------|

This piece sacrifice is essentially desperation.

| 22 | ...  | ♖xb6 |
|----|------|------|
| 23 | bxc5 | ♖c6  |
| 24 | ♖a5  | ♘e5  |
| 25 | ♘f4  | ♕g5  |
| 26 | ♕d4  | ♖b8  |
| 27 | ♖a1  | h6   |
| 28 | ♖xa6 |      |

The only way to get castled is to give up a full rook, but this merely demonstrates the bankruptcy of White's position.

| 28 | ...  | ♖xa6 |
|----|------|------|
| 29 | 0-0  | ♘c6  |
| 30 | ♕c4  | ♖a5  |
|    | 0-1  |      |

As an advertisement for Black's strategy this game is brilliant. There are few black defences available nowadays which can reduce White to rubble so rapidly.

For a full analysis of this line see chapter five.

## Through the Looking Glass

And what if White accepts the challenge and chases Black's provocative knight? Two-times world title contender, Efim Bogoljubow, demonstrated Black's resources in this Mirror Alekhine Defence line.

Game 2
**Weinitschke-Bogoljubow**
*Elster 1938*

| | 1 | d4 | ♘c6 |
| | 2 | d5 | ♘e5 |
| | 3 | f4 | |

White treats the opening as a kind of mirror image to Alekhine's defence, with Black's queen's knight being hounded to the other side of the board. However, the difference is that here White weakens his kingside by striving excessively to underline the reflective analogy.

| | 3 | ... | ♘g6 |
| | 4 | e4 | e5 |

This tactical resource emphasises the difference. The parallel move ...d5 is not an option in the Alekhine Defence, viz. 1 e4 ♘f6 2 e5 ♘d5 3 c4 ♘b6 4 d4 d5? 5 c5 when Black is already cramped and suffering severely. As we shall see in this game, White gets into trouble by trying to repeat this line move for move on the opposite wing.

4...e6 is seen in modern play, e.g. Gerusel-Miles, Porz 1982, a drastic miniature; 5 ♘f3 exd5 6 exd5 ♗c5 7 ♕d3 d6 8 ♗e2 ♘f6

9 ♘c3 0-0 10 ♗d2 ♘g4 11 ♘d1 ♖e8 12 h3 ♘f6 13 g4 ♘e4 14 ♖h2 ♘h4 15 ♘g5 ♘xg5 16 fxg5 ♕e7 17 ♕g3 (now Black wins material with an astounding stroke! See page 114 for an amusing parallel) 17...♗g1

18 ♖f2 ♗xf2+ 19 ♕xf2 ♕e4 20 ♘e3 ♕h1+ 21 ♗f1 ♘f3+ 22 ♔d1 ♘xg5 0-1.

| | 5 | f5 | |

Optimistically hoping for a supine retreat, 5...♘6e7, when White's space advantage would be immense. More cautious would be 5 dxe6 though after 5...fxe6 Black has the open f-file as a base for counter-attack. See page 114 for analysis.

| | 5 | ... | ♕h4+ |

Naturally Black chooses a more active continuation, even though it involves the sacrifice of material.

| | 6 | ♔d2 | ♕xe4 |

Not 6...♘f4 7 g3 or 6...♘ge7 7 ♘c3 to be followed by ♘f3, gaining time and space, when White's opening play would

have been justified. This carries the fight to the opponent.

**7 fxg6**

If 7 ♗d3 Black can respond 7...♕xg2+ 8 ♘e2 ♕g5+ 9 ♔c3 ♕h4 Ulrich-Bogoljubow, Elster 1937.

| 7 | ... | ♕xd5+ |
|---|-----|-------|
| 8 | ♔e1 | ♕xd1+ |
| 9 | ♔xd1 | hxg6 |
| 10 | ♘c3 | c6 |
| 11 | ♘f3 | f6 |
| 12 | ♗d3 | |

Storing up trouble. White's minor pieces become potentially exposed to the advancing black pawns. In order to make a game of it White had to play 12 ♗e2.

| 12 | ... | ♘e7 |
|----|-----|-----|
| 13 | ♖e1 | d5 |

Black's opening sacrifice has been a complete success. He controls the centre and his three pawns outweigh White's extra piece. White now decides to return this piece, but this is a somewhat forlorn gesture.

| 14 | h3 | e4 |
|----|-----|------|
| 15 | ♗xe4 | dxe4 |
| 16 | ♘xe4 | ♔f7 |

| 17 | ♗d2 | |

If 17 ♘d6+ then simply 17...♔g8 when Black's king is safe.

| | | |
|---|---|---|
| 17 | ... | ♘f5 |
| 18 | b3 | g5 |
| 19 | ♔e2 | ♘d6 |
| 20 | ♘f2 | ♗f5 |
| 21 | ♘d4 | ♗g6 |
| 22 | ♔f1 | ♘f5 |
| 23 | ♘e2 | ♗c5 |
| 24 | ♘e4 | ♗b6 |

Black's task is easy. He has an extra pawn, two bishops and better development.

| | | |
|---|---|---|
| 25 | c4 | ♖ad8 |
| 26 | ♖ed1 | ♖xd2 |
| 27 | ♘xd2 | ♘e3+ |
| | 0-1 | |

White resigns on account of 28 ♔e1 ♘xg2+ 29 ♔f1 ♘e3+ 30 ♔e1 ♖xh3.

A splendid example of the dynamism concealed in the black opening.

For a full analysis of this line see chapter four.

**Ducking the Challenge**

What if White ducks out of the challenge with 1 d4 ♘c6 2 ♘f3? Bogoljubow used to play 2...g6. Here, however, we recommend transposition to the Chigorin Defence, 1 d4 d5 2 c4 ♘c6!?, but without giving White the option of the dangerous 1 d4 d5 2 c4 ♘c6 3 ♘c3!.

This unusual defence has the virtue that it can score remarkably quick wins against unprepared opposition. The Russian grandmaster Mikhail Chigorin

was the first to adopt it, and he amassed a number of very rapid knockouts with it against unsuspecting opponents. In recent years, it has also proved popular with Nigel Short. Here are some of the classic examples by the line's inventor.

Game 3
**Teichmann - Chigorin**
*Cambridge Springs 1904*

| | | |
|---|---|---|
| 1 | d4 | ♘c6 |
| 2 | ♘f3 | d5 |

Readers should note that in all games, we have standardised the opening sequence as 1 d4 ♘c6 2 ♘f3 d5, even though several may have reached the critical positions by transposition via 1 d4 d5 2 c4 ♘c6.

| | | |
|---|---|---|
| 3 | c4 | ♗g4 |

Now Black has the position he wants. Here White could try 4 ♘c3 ♗xf3 5 gxf3 e6 6 e3 ♗b4 7 cxd5 ♕xd5 8 ♗d2 ♗xc3 9 bxc3 though after 9...♘ge7, in the game Lasker-Chigorin, Hastings 1895, Black's pair of knights give him good counterplay. Another possibility is 4 ♘c3 e6 5 ♗g5 ♗e7 6 ♗xe7 ♘gxe7 7 cxd5 ♘xd5 8 e3 0-0 9 ♗e2 ♘xc3 10 bxc3 ♘a5 11 ♕a4 b6 Hulak-Muse, Vinkovci 1993 when Black has a solid position. In fact, Black won both of these games. Finally, 4 e3 e6 5 ♘c3 ♗b4 6 ♗d2 ♘ge7 7 ♗d3 ♗f5 8 ♗xf5 ♘xf5 9 cxd5 exd5 10 ♕b3 ♗xc3 11 ♗xc3 ♖b8 with a level position as in Steinitz-Chigorin, World Championship, Game 12, Havana 1889. See page 128 for our recommendations.

| 4 | cxd5 | ♗xf3 |
|---|------|------|
| 5 | dxc6 | ♗xc6 |
| 6 | ♘c3 | e6 |

| 7 | ♗f4 |
|---|-----|

In the next game we shall look at the more testing 7 e4.

| 7 | ... | ♘f6 |
|----|------|------|
| 8 | e3 | ♗b4 |
| 9 | ♕b3 | ♘d5 |
| 10 | ♗g3 | 0-0 |
| 11 | ♗d3 | ♕g5 |

With this move Black seizes the initiative and maintains it until the end of the game. The point is that if 12 0-0, then 12...♗xc3 13 bxc3 ♘xe3 wins material.

| 12 | ♕c2 | f5 |
|----|-----|----|
| 13 | ♗e5 | |

Hoping that Black will snatch the bait on g2 but he does not oblige.

| 13 | ... | ♖f7 |
|----|-------|-----|
| 14 | 0-0-0 | ♗xc3 |
| 15 | bxc3 | b5 |

Black's attack spreads to the other wing and White is soon overwhelmed.

| 16 | ♖hg1 | ♕e7 |
|----|------|------|
| 17 | ♖df1 | ♕a3+ |
| 18 | ♔d2 | b4 |
| 19 | c4 | |

After this, Black's pieces pour in but clearly 19 cxb4 ♘xb4 is a disaster for White.

| 19 | ... | ♗a4 |
|----|------|------|
| 20 | ♕b1 | ♘c3 |
| 21 | ♕a1 | ♖d8 |
| 22 | g3 | ♘e4+ |
| 23 | ♔e2 | ♘c5 |

**24    ♕b1**

Not 24 dxc5 ♕xd3+ or 24 ♗b1 ♘b3 spectacularly winning White's queen.

|    | **24** | **...** | **♘xd3** |
|----|----|----|----|
|    | **25** | **♕xd3** | **♕xa2+** |
|    | **26** | **♔f3** | **♗c2** |

**0-1**

White's queen still goes, e.g. 27 ♕e2 ♗e4+ or 27 ♕d2 ♗e4+ 28 ♔e2 ♗f3+. White therefore resigned. There are few openings in which Black can score quite so quickly and decisively.

### Game 4
### Pillsbury - Chigorin
*St Petersburg 1896*

| **1** | **d4** | **♘c6** |
|----|----|----|
| **2** | **♘f3** | **d5** |
| **3** | **c4** | **♗g4** |
| **4** | **cxd5** | **♗xf3** |
| **5** | **dxc6** | |

Or 5 gxf3 ♕xd5 6 e3 0-0-0! 7 ♘c3 ♕h5 8 ♗d2 ♘f6 9 f4 ♕xd1+ 10 ♖xd1 e6 11 ♗g2 when 11...♘e7, followed by ...♘d5, gave Black an excellent

central fortress in Christiansen-Short, Monaco (blindfold) 1993. Black's later plan is to expand with ...h6, ...f5 and ...g5.

**5    ...    ♗xc6**

**6    ♘c3    e6**

A fascinating gambit occurs after 6...♘f6 7 f3 e5! 8 dxe5 ♕xd1+ 9 ♔xd1 ♘d7 10 f4 0-0-0 11 ♔c2 ♗c5 and ...♖he8, with full value for the pawn.

**7    e4**

This is the first divergence from the previous game.

**7    ...    ♗b4**
**8    f3    f5**

A risky and ambitious attempt to batter White's centre into submission.

**9  e5**

Now Black overruns the board. White must gambit himself here with 9 ♗c4! fxe4 10 0-0 exf3 11 ♗xe6 fxg2 12 ♖e1.

| | | |
|---|---|---|
| 9 | ... | ♘e7 |
| 10 | a3 | ♗a5 |
| 11 | ♗c4 | ♗d5 |
| 12 | ♕a4+ | c6 |
| 13 | ♗d3 | ♕b6 |

Threatening an immediate win with ...♗b3, netting the White queen.

| | | |
|---|---|---|
| 14 | ♗c2 | ♕a6 |

Now with a new threat of ...b5, winning White's queen.

**15  ♗d1?**

After this White is smashed. 15 b4! ♕c4 16 ♗b2 was the last chance.

| | | |
|---|---|---|
| 15 | ... | ♗c4 |
| 16 | f4 | 0-0-0 |
| 17 | ♗e3 | ♘d5 |
| 18 | ♗d2 | ♘b6 |
| 19 | ♕c2 | ♖xd4 |
| 20 | ♖c1 | ♗d3 |

| | | |
|---|---|---|
| 21 | ♕b3 | ♘c4 |

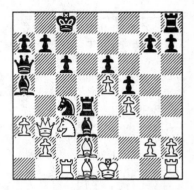

Winning a piece. The rest is agony.

| | | |
|---|---|---|
| 22 | ♔f2 | ♘xd2 |
| 23 | ♕xe6+ | ♔b8 |
| 24 | ♗f3 | ♕b6 |
| 25 | ♔g3 | ♘xf3 |
| 26 | gxf3 | ♗c4 |
| 27 | ♕xf5 | ♗xc3 |
| 28 | bxc3 | ♖d2 |
| 29 | ♕h3 | g6 |
| 30 | ♔h4 | h6 |
| 31 | ♕g4 | ♕f2+ |
| 32 | ♕g3 | g5+ |
| 33 | ♔g4 | h5+ |
| 34 | ♔f5 | ♗d3+ |
| 35 | ♔e6 | ♕b6 |
| 36 | ♕xg5 | c5+ |
| 37 | ♔f7 | ♗c4+ |
| 38 | ♔g7 | ♖g8+ |

**0-1**

After 39 ♔h7 ♖d7+ 40 ♕g7 ♖dxg7 we have, as a contemporary note put it, 'A very pronounced case of checkmate indeed.'

For our detailed analysis of this variation see page 124.

## Section B
## Against 1 e4

We have seen Bogoljubow and Chigorin in action against the opening move 1 d4. Both of these grandmasters were twice contenders for the World Championship. The man who put 1...♘c6 on the map against 1 e4 was the great chess thinker and strategist, Aron Nimzowitsch, author of *My System* and arguably world number two to World Champion Alekhine at the close of the 1920s and the opening of the 1930s. Here are some of his classic masterpieces with the defence he introduced and regularly championed.

We start with Nimzowitsch's most impressive win with 1...♘c6.

### Game 5
### Spielmann-Nimzowitsch
*Stockholm 1920*

| | | |
|---|---|---|
| 1 | e4 | ♘c6 |
| 2 | d4 | d5!? |

The pure, Nimzowitschian interpretation of this defence which normally leads to intricate pawn chain play. When this defence is employed in contemporary chess 2...e5 tends to be preferred and it is the line we recommend too, on account of 2...d5 3 ♘c3!. For our analysis of 2...e5 see chapter two.

| | | |
|---|---|---|
| 3 | e5 | |

One might have expected the more fluid 3 ♘c3!? from Spielmann which is, in fact, the best move.

| | | |
|---|---|---|
| 3 | ... | ♗f5 |

An even more provocative method of handling this provocative defence is 3...f6!?.

| | | |
|---|---|---|
| 4 | ♘e2?! | |

Better is 4 ♘f3!?. The plan chosen by White diverts too many pieces from the protection of his centre (d4) and could have boomeranged seriously had Black played correctly on move 7.

| | | |
|---|---|---|
| 4 | ... | e6 |
| 5 | ♘g3 | ♗g6 |
| 6 | h4 | h5 |
| 7 | ♗e2 *(D)* | |
| 7 | ... | ♗e7?! |

Inviting remarkable complications. Instead of this flank defence to White's pressure against his h-pawn it was possible to obtain a fine position by means of a central counterattack, as suggested later by Nimzowitsch: thus 7...♘b4! 8 ♘a3 c5 9 c3 ♘c6 10 ♘xh5

♗xh5 11 ♗xh5 cxd4 12 cxd4
♗b4+ 13 ♔f1 ♗xa3 14 bxa3 g6
15 ♗e2 ♖xh4 16 ♖xh4 ♕xh4
threatening mate and the d-
pawn.

| 8 | ♗xh5 | ♗xh5 |
|----|------|------|
| 9 | ♘xh5 | g6 |
| 10 | ♘f4 | ♖xh4 |
| 11 | ♖xh4 | ♗xh4 |
| 12 | ♕d3 | |

**12 ... ♘ge7!!**
Surely Black must now lose
material?
**13 g3 ♘f5**
13...♗g5 would lose to the
trap 14 ♘xe6, so the text is

forced. The remarkable move,
then, was Black's 12th which
prepared this combination.
White could decline Black's
'passive' sacrifice with 14 c3,
allowing ...♗g5 at last, but why
should he? Is it obvious that
Black obtains anything concrete
for his sacrificed piece?
**14 gxh4 ♘fxd4**
The compensation to date
amounts to one pawn, but more
is to come, since the founda-
tions of White's pawn centre
have been destroyed. The
threats at the moment (positive-
ly crude in comparison with the
enchanting variations based on
the power of his centralised
knight pair which Nimzowitsch
soon conjures up) are 15...♘b4
16 ♕xd4 ♘xc2+ and 15...♘xe5
16 ♕xe5 ♘f3+.

**15 ♘a3 ♕xh4**
Rejecting the possibility of
entering an endgame where he
would possess three pawns for a
piece. This possibility arises
after 15...♘xe5 16 ♕h3 ♘df3+

17 ♔f1 ♛xh4. In this case it would certainly be Black who would be justified in playing for a win. However, Nimzowitsch had observed a variation of truly shattering beauty.

**16   ♛h3   ♛g5?!**

It was still possible to steer for an ending which promised a good possibility of victory (16...♛xh3 17 ♘xh3 ♘xe5 18 ♗f4 ♘ef3+). With the text Nimzowitsch subordinates his desire for the accumulation of points to his desire for the creation of beauty.

**17   ♗e3?**

This is a plausible move which, however, loses spectacularly. The line conceived by Nimzowitsch ran as follows: 17 ♛h8+ ♔d7 18 ♛xa8 ♛g1+ 19 ♔d2 ♛xf2+ 20 ♔c3 *(see following diagram)* and now both 20...♘f3 and the amazing 20...♘b3 force a black win.

White's best is 17 ♘d3!, when Black should play quietly with 17...0-0-0! when his pros-

pects are still not bad. He is ahead in development with two pawns for a piece and with White somewhat tied up.

**17   ...   ♛g1+**
**18   ♛f1**

Or 18 ♔d2 ♛xa1 19 ♛h8+ ♔d7 20 ♛xa8 ♛xb2! winning.

**18   ...   ♘f3+**
**19   ♔e2   ♘fd4+**
**20   ♔d2   ♘f3+**
**21   ♔e2   ♘cd4+**

No draw.

**22   ♔d3?**

The losing error. It was essential to eliminate one of the

knights with the capture 22 ♗xd4. Admittedly the continuation 22...♘xd4+ 23 ♔d3 ♕g5 24 ♔xd4 ♕xf4+ 25 ♔d3 c5 is unpleasant for White, but it was obligatory to continue thus if White wanted to resist.

| 22 | ... | ♕g5 |
|---|---|---|
| 23 | ♕h3 | ♕xe5 |
| 24 | ♖f1 | 0-0-0 |

Now that Black has completed his development White is helpless. This position should be preserved for the benefit of posterity.

| 25 | b3 | b5 |
|---|---|---|
| 26 | ♘xb5 | ♕e4+ |
| 27 | ♔c3 | ♕xc2+ |
| 28 | ♔b4 | c5+ |
| | 0-1 | |

**Again Ducking the Challenge**
What to do if White side-steps the challenge with 2 ♘f3, hoping for 2...e5 3 ♗b5 with a conventional Ruy Lopez? In chapter three we propose Tony Miles's favourite 2...d6. Nimzowitsch tried something play-

able, but riskier, in another game against the highly inventive Austrian grandmaster Rudolf Spielmann.

Game 6
**Spielmann-Nimzowitsch**
*New York 1927*

| 1 | e4 | ♘c6 |
|---|---|---|
| 2 | ♘f3 | e6 |
| 3 | d4 | d5 |
| 4 | e5 | |

Transposing to a version of the French Defence where Black will experience problems in undermining White's centre by means of ...c5.

| 4 | ... | b6 |
|---|---|---|

'Since Black cannot make any progress without ...c5 I would try here 4...♘a5!? and only after 5 c3 would I continue with 5...b6' (Alekhine).

| 5 | c3 | ♘ce7!? |
|---|---|---|

The start of a rather artificial manoeuvre designed to seize control of the f5-square. Black seems to have abandoned all respect for the hallowed clichés concerning development.

**6  ♗d3    a5**

Hoping to exchange his light-squared bishop, but White forestalls this.

**7  ♕e2    ♘f5**
**8  h4     h5**
**9  ♘g5    g6**

'Black's position could, perhaps, have withstood the eccentricities committed so far, since they did not create any irreparable weaknesses in his own camp. However, this frightful weakening of f6 - given the absence of any stable and effective strong points for his own pieces - transforms his situation into a hopeless one' (Alekhine).

Nimzowitsch later recommended 9...♘ge7 as better, e.g. 10 ♘d2 c5, and 11 ♘f1 is impossible as the d-pawn hangs.

**10  ♘d2    ♘ge7**

And not 10...♘xh4? 11 ♗b5+ but 10...c5 looks stronger.

**11  ♘f1**

Protecting his g3-square and thus preparing to force the withdrawal of Black's knight by means of c3 and g4. If Nimzowitsch's plan was to restrain White's kingside pawns it has clearly been a failure.

**11  ...    c5**
**12  f3     c4**

Or 12...cxd4 13 g4 hxg4 14 fxg4 ♘xh4 15 ♕f2 winning outright. The advance of the text is characteristic of Nimzowitsch in that he renounces the attack against the frontal area of the white pawn-chain, preferring to transfer his onslaught to the base (c3 and b2). Furthermore the struggle in this game has clearly been subdivided into two theatres of war by the very nature of the pawn-chain. 12...c4 ensures that Black will retain a valuable spatial advantage on the queenside if White fails to burst through on the opposite wing.

**13  ♗c2    b5**
**14  g4     ♘g7**

An unusual fianchetto of the Black queen's knight on the g7-square!

**15  ♘g3    ♘c6**

And that is the king's knight. Black has played six moves out of fifteen with his knights and not yet touched any of his other pieces.

**16  ♕g2    ♗e7**

On 16...♖a7 Alekhine gives: 17 gxh5 ♘xh5 18 ♘xh5 ♖xh5 19 ♘xf7 ♖xf7 20 ♗xg6 ♖xh4 21 ♗xf7+ ♔xf7 22 ♖g1.

**17  gxh5    gxh5**

17...♘xh5 is positionally correct but tactically faulty: 18 ♘xh5 ♖xh5 19 ♘xf7 and Black can resign.

**18  ♖g1**

18 ♘h7 would have been very strong, with the threat of 19 ♘f6+ ♗xf6 20 exf6 ♕xf6 21 ♗g5 neatly trapping Black's queen. If in reply 18...♗xh4, then 19 ♖xh4! ♕xh4 20 ♗g5 is still decisive.

The text should, in fact, win, but the correct follow-up is not easy to find. Alekhine gives the preparatory 19 ♔e2!, which maintains the option of sacrificing on f7, while eliminating any counterplay (e.g. checks on h4).

**19  ...    ♔xf7**
**20  ♘xh5?**

Alekhine mentions four plausible alternatives which White had to analyse: 20 ♗g6+, 20 ♘e4, 20 ♘f5 and 20 ♘e2. The strongest of these is 20 ♘e2 ♗xh4+ 21 ♔d1 ♕g8 22 ♘f4 ♖f7 23 ♘g6 ♗e7 24 ♘xh8 ♔xh8 25 ♕g6! and wins!

**20  ...    ♗xh4+**
**21  ♔e2    ♘xh5**
**22  ♗g6+   ♔e7**
**23  ♗xh5**

**23  ...    ♔d7!**

Spielmann had overlooked this, expecting only 23...♖xh5 24 ♕g7+ ♔e8 25 ♕g6+, which is most unpleasant for Black. After the text it is Black who is winning.

**18  ...    ♖a7**
**19  ♘xf7!?**

| 24 | ♕g7+ | ♗e7 |
|----|------|-----|
| 25 | ♗f7 | ♖h2+ |
| 26 | ♔d1 | ♔c7 |

The base of White's pawn-chain falls in a highly unexpected manner.

| 27 | ♗f4 | ♖xb2 |
|----|------|------|
| 28 | ♕h7 | ♔b6 |
| 29 | ♖g8 | ♕c7 |
| 30 | ♕h8 | ♞d8 |
| 31 | ♗g6 | ♖g2 |
| 32 | ♕h1 | |

Once White is compelled to retreat the end is in sight.

| 32 | ... | ♖xg6 |
|----|-----|------|

Over the next few moves Black cashes in his material plus in return for a decisive initiative.

| 33 | ♖xg6 | b4 |
|----|------|------|
| 34 | ♖g7 | ♕c6 |
| 35 | ♕h8 | ♕a4+ |
| 36 | ♔e1 | ♞c6 |
| 37 | ♕xc8 | ♗h4+ |
| 38 | ♗g3 | |

Or 38 ♖g3 ♕c2 with annihilating effect.

| 38 | ... | ♖xg7 |
|----|-----|------|
| 39 | ♗xh4 | |

This re-establishes material equality.

| 39 | ... | ♕c2! |
|----|-----|------|

Avoiding the trap 39...♖g1+ 40 ♔f2 ♖xa1 41 ♗d8+! ♞xd8 42 ♕xd8+ when White secures perpetual check.

| 40 | ♗d8+ | ♞xd8 |
|----|------|------|

| 41 | ♕b8+ | 0-1 |
|----|------|-----|

In this case 41 ♕xd8+ ♔b7 is quite hopeless. Black threatens mate and the rook, while the g7-rook defends the black king from the checks.

Those notes to this game mentioned as stemming from Alekhine we have translated from his tournament book, in German, of New York, 1927. Exciting stuff, but we cannot honestly recommend readers to play this riskily as Black. For our recommendation against 2 ♞f3 see chapter three.

**The Main Test**
Also testing for Black are lines based on ♞c3 particularly, if Black insists on playing ...d5.

Game 7
**Brinckmann-Nimzowitsch**
*Niendorf 1927*
(Notes based on those by Reti)

**1  e4     ♘c6
2  ♘c3**

In an absolute sense, this move is hardly a very strong one as Black can, with 2...e5, bring about the innocuous Vienna Game. Relatively, however, i.e. against Nimzowitsch, the move does have this advantage over an immediate 2 d4, that Black being anxious to play ...d5 plays the preparatory move 2...e6 whereupon his queen's bishop can no longer develop at f5.

**2  ...    e6
3  d4     d5**

Also worth considering is 3...♗b4 as Nimzowitsch played in two games against Maroczy: 4 ♗e3 ♘ge7 5 ♕g4 0-0 6 ♕h4 f5 7 f3 d5 8 e5 ♘a5 9 a3 ♗xc3+ 10 bxc3 ♕e8 11 ♘h3 ♘c4, Maroczy-Nimzowitsch, Karlsbad 1923 or 4 ♘f3 d6 5 ♗f4 ♘ge7 6 ♗e2 ♗xc3+ 7 bxc3 0-0 8 0-0 ♘g6 9 ♗e3 ♕e7 10 ♖e1 ♗d7 11 ♕c1 b6 12 ♘d2 e5 Maroczy-Nimzowitsch, San Remo 1930. There is plenty of scope for originality in this line.

**4  e5**

This move can be made here with less hesitation than in the analogous variations of the French Defence, as Black cannot clean up White's centre

with ...c5 so easily, on account of the knight at c6.

**4  ...    ♘ge7
5  ♘f3    b6
6  ♘e2**

White wants to have the possibility of consolidating his centre with c3, but thereby makes possible for his opponent the following strong move, which eventually leads to the exchange of Black's inactive queen's bishop for White's king's bishop, which has much more scope.

**6  ...    ♗a6
7  ♘g3    ♗xf1
8  ♔xf1**

White has plans for attack, and therefore does not want to go back with his knight.

**8  ...    h5!**

Such manoeuvres are somewhat startling, and yet they are excellent, and aim at the domination of light squares. First there is a threat of ...h4; combined with an impregnable knight position on f5. We shall see later that, positionally, the most important factor in this game is Black's domination of the light squares, which has been made possible only by the exchange of White's king's bishop.

| 9 | ♗g5 | ♛c8 |
| 10 | ♛d3 | |

White wants to meet the thrust ...♛a6. Positionally more correct, however, would be to maintain the knight on g3 by h4.

| 10 | ... | ♞g6 |
| 11 | c3 | |

Even now White could still play h4, but then Black could seize the initiative on the queenside by gaining time with ...♞b4 and ...c5.

| 11 | ... | h4 |
| 12 | ♞e2 | ♗e7 |
| 13 | h3 | ♗xg5 |
| 14 | ♞xg5 | ♞ce7 *(D)* |

Much profit can be derived from a study of this position. White is in control of more territory, and so one might think

he has the advantage. But that is not the case. The real criterion by which to appraise close positions is the possibility of breaking through. In general, the player who can move freely over a greater area can probably place his pieces more advantageously for a possible breakthrough than his opponent, who is restricted in his movements.

As we know, this is the idea underlying the method of playing in restricted positions which owes so much to Dr Tarrasch. Tarrasch's opposite, Nimzowitsch, now shows that one may be in a restricted position and yet have every possibility of breaking through. Thus, in the present position, the possibilities of White's breaking through obviously lie in c4, and f4-f5. The first is scarcely a strong move, for White dominates more territory in the middle and on the kingside, but not on the queenside. In the present case it is a particularly doubtful move, as White's d-pawn would become backward. The liberating move dictated by the position would therefore be f4-f5.

But there can be no question of making these moves, as White will obviously never be able to dominate the f5-square. Furthermore, Black has made a very good provision for the future in his seemingly artificial but really very profound manoeuvres (...♘g6, ...h5-h4, ...♘e7, but above all in the exchange of White's king's bishop).

Thus, while White has no serious possibilities of breaking through, and is therefore limited to making waiting moves behind the wall of his pawns, the second player has at his disposal the possibilities of breaking through afforded him by ...f6 and ...c5. Black alone, therefore, is able to take the initiative, and consequently he is in a superior position, in spite of his limited territory.

| 15 | ♔g1 | f6 |
|----|-----|-----|
| 16 | ♘f3 | ♕d7 |
| 17 | ♔h2 | c5 |
| 18 | c4 | |

Surprising, but as Brinckmann himself states in the Niendorf tournament book, he commits an act of violence in this move, realising that otherwise he will be gradually crushed through lack of counterplay. However, by opening up the game like this, he is playing into Black's hands.

| 18 | ... | ♕c7 |
|----|-----|-----|
| 19 | cxd5 | c4 |
| 20 | ♕c2 | exd5 |
| 21 | ♖he1 | 0–0 |
| 22 | ♘c3 | fxe5 |
| 23 | ♘xe5 | ♘xe5 |
| 24 | dxe5 | d4 |
| 25 | ♘b5 | ♕c5 |
| 26 | ♘d6 | d3 |

It would seem simpler for Black to keep his mass of pawns intact with 26...b5. However, White will reply with 27 ♕d2, and obtain counter chances on the kingside, where he has the superiority.

| 27 | ♕xc4+ | ♕xc4 |
|----|-------|------|
| 28 | ♘xc4 | ♖xf2 |
| 29 | ♖ad1 | ♖c8 |
| 30 | ♘e3 | ♖d8 |
| 31 | ♘c4 | ♘f5 |

After an immediate 31...b5 there would follow 32 ♘d6. But now White must prevent ...b5.

**32    a4**

In reply to 32 e6 Nimzowitsch planned the beautiful reply 32...♖e2. If then 33 ♖xd3, for example, there would follow 33...♖xe1 34 ♖xd8+ ♔h7 and White has no defence against the threat ...♘g3.

| 32 | ... | ♔f7 |
|----|-----|-----|
| 33 | ♖e4 | ♖e2! |

**34    ♖f4**

White is now completely lost. After 34 ♖xe2 dxe2 35 Re1, Black would win with 35...♖d1 36 ♖xe2 ♘g3.

| 34 | ... | ♔e6 |
|----|-----|-----|
| 35 | ♖g4 | d2 |
| 36 | ♖g6+ | ♔f7 |
| 37 | ♖g4 | a6 |
| 38 | ♖f4 | ♔e6 |

White now has no defence against ...g5.

| 39 | ♘d6 | ♘e3 |
|----|-----|-----|
|    | **0–1** |  |

However, the attempt to play more fluidly against ♘c3 had also proved to be dangerous.

### Game 8
### Wendel-Nimzowitsch
*Stockholm 1921*

| 1 | e4 | ♘c6 |
|---|-----|------|
| 2 | d4 | d5 |
| 3 | ♘c3 | |

One of the sharpest methods of combating Nimzowitsch's special defence. With this move White offers a pawn sacrifice in order to destroy Black's strong point on d5. In this case Nimzowitsch accepts the challenge.

**3    ...    dxe4**

The alternative is the stolid refusal to give ground 3...e6. Later in the 1920s (as in the Brinckmann game we have just seen) Nimzowitsch gained many victories with this move, one other of which is sufficiently amusing to merit reproduction here: Mieses-Nimzowitsch, Kissingen 1928: 3...e6 4 exd5 exd5 5 ♗e3 ♗f5 6 ♗d3 ♘ge7 7 ♘ge2 ♘b4 8 ♗xf5 ♘xf5 9 ♗f4 g5 10 ♗d2 ♗e7 11 ♕c1 f6 12 ♘d1 ♘c6 13 c3 ♘h4 14 ♘e3 ♕d7 15 ♕c2 f5 16 f4 0-0-0 17 0-0-0 ♖hf8 18 ♖df1 ♖de8 19 fxg5 ♗xg5 20 ♘f4 ♘e7 21 ♔b1 ♗xf4 22 ♖xf4 ♘eg6 23 ♖f2 f4 24 ♘d1 ♕g4 25 ♗c1 ♘f5 26 ♖hf1 ♘d6 27 h3 ♕g5 28 ♖e2 ♖e4 29 ♖ef2 ♖fe8 30 ♕d3 ♘f5 31 ♖g1 ♘g3 32 ♗d2 ♕f5 33 a3 ♕e6 34 ♔a1 ♕c6 35 ♕f3 h5 36 ♔a2 ♕b5 (completing the encirclement) 37 ♔a1 (*see following diagram*) 37...♘h4 checkmate, but to White's queen rather than his king!

**4    d5**

And not 4 ♗b5? ♗d7 5 ♘xe4 ♘xd4! winning a pawn in broad daylight.

**4    ...    ♘e5**

4...♘b8 is possible but such a retrograde move is hardly in the spirit of the opening.

**5    ♗f4    ♘g6**
**6    ♗g3**

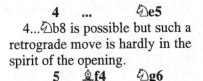

**6    ...    a6**

Black naturally has to prevent ♘b5 and the obvious way to achieve this is 6...f5 but then 7 ♘h3! with a big plus for White and Black has great difficulty in freeing his position, e.g. 7...e5 8 dxe6 ♕xd1+ (8...♗xe6 9 ♘b5 ♗b4+ 10 c3 ♗a5 11 ♕a4 ♗b6 12 ♘xc7+ ♔f7 13 ♖d1 ♗xc7

14 ♖xd8 ♗xd8 15 ♗c4 ♘f8 16 ♘f4 ♘f6 17 ♘xe6 ♘xe6 18 ♕b3 1-0 Borngaesser-Louis, Bundesliga 1982) 9 ♖xd1 c6 (9...♗b4 10 ♗c4 ♔e7 11 0-0 ♗xc3 12 bxc3 ♗xe6 13 ♗xe6 ♔xe6 14 f3 h6 15 fxe4 fxe4 16 ♘f2 with a powerful attack, P. Nielsen-Furhoff, Copenhagen 1991) 10 ♗c4 h6 11 0-0 ♘f6 12 f3 ♗c5+ 13 ♔h1 b5 14 ♗b3 e3 15 ♖fe1 ♔e7 16 ♘f4 ♘xf4 17 ♗xf4 ♗a6 18 ♘e2 ♖ad8 19 ♖xd8 ♔xd8 20 ♗e5 and the pawn on e6 remains a bone in Black's throat, Apicella-Soetewey, Brussels Z 1993.

**7 f3?!**

Much stronger is Boleslavsky's 7 ♗c4 ♘f6 8 ♕e2 ♗f5 9 0–0–0. White's choice in the game permits Nimzowitsch to return his extra pawn for a lasting initiative. Our conclusion must be that the whole line with 3...dxe4 is suspect.

| 7 | ... | f5 |
|---|-----|-----|
| 8 | fxe4 | f4 |
| 9 | ♗f2 | e5 |

**10 ♘f3**

10 dxe6 ♗xe6 would give Black a splendid development and leave White with a weak e-pawn.

**10 ... ♗d6**

'A move dictated by the law of the blockade: passed and semi-passed pawns must be blockaded' (Nimzowitsch). Nimzowitsch regarded this position as approximately level and considered that White's next moves should have been ♗d3, 0-0 and ♘e2, followed by the activation of his queenside majority c4-c5. As it is, White fails to spot this plan and indulges, instead, in a series of highly artificial manoeuvres.

**11 h4?**

Black's next is the first step in the plan to restrain White's advance of c4.

| 11 | ... | b5 |
|----|------|------|
| 12 | h5 | ♘f8 |
| 13 | ♗h4 | ♕d7 |
| 14 | ♗e2 | b4 |
| 15 | ♘b1 | ♘f6 |

Threatening White's e-pawn and h-pawn. White has but one method of avoiding material loss.

**16 ♗xf6**

Unpleasant but forced. After this exchange Black's centre is strengthened and he is given the open g-file as a free gift in which to operate against White's weak g-pawn. On top of this the absence of White's queen's bishop leaves him woefully exposed on the dark squares. From now on White is reduced to meeting Black's threats and can form no positive schemes of his own.

| 16 | ... | gxf6 |
|----|------|------|
| 17 | ♘bd2 | ♕g7 |
| 18 | ♔f1 | ♘d7 |
| 19 | h6 | ♕g3 |
| 20 | ♖h3 | ♕g8 |
| 21 | ♘h4 | ♘c5 |
| 22 | ♖h1 | ♖b8 |
| 23 | c3?! | |

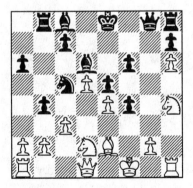

A weird reaction to Black's last move, which was obviously conceived as a prophylactic measure against 23 c3. Black now seizes the b-file in addition to his other treasures.

| 23 | ... | bxc3 |
|----|------|------|
| 24 | bxc3 | ♕g3 |
| 25 | ♕c2 | ♖g8 |
| 26 | ♘c4 | ♗d7 |
| 27 | ♘xd6+ | cxd6 |
| 28 | ♗f3 | |

In control of all the open lines and all the dark squares and with White's units strewn at random around the perimeters of the battle-field Black has an obviously winning position. The positional way to victory, pointed out by Nimzowitsch, was 28...♔d8 29 ♘f5 ♗xf5 30 exf5 ♖e8 31 ♖h3 ♕g8! and White's position is an uncoordinated shambles.

But, as so often, Nimzowitsch espies a combination which leads even more rapidly to the desired goal. And, as we might expect, this combination is laced with problem moves. It almost looks like a constructed situation rather than a game continuation. Black to play and win; it is certainly worthwhile trying to find Nimzowitsch's beautiful win yourself before inspecting the remainder of the game.

| 28 | ... | ♗b5+ |
|----|-----|------|
| 29 | c4 | ♗xc4+ |
| 30 | ♕xc4 | ♖b2 |
| 31 | ♗e2 | ♖g4 |
| 32 | ♕c1 | |

32 ♖h3 looks like an adequate defence, but then comes the brilliant stroke 32...♖xh4!, e.g. 33 ♖xg3 ♖h1+ 34 ♔f2 fxg3+ 35 ♔xg3 ♖xa1. 'Black wins the a-pawn and then decides the game in his favour by a direct attack with the rooks. Do not overlook that passed black a-pawn lurking in the background' (Nimzowitsch).

| 32 | ... | ♖xh4 |
|----|-----|------|
| 33 | ♖xh4 | ♖xe2! |
| 34 | ♔xe2 | ♕xg2+ |

As in his game versus Spielmann from Stockholm 1920 (page 18), Nimzowitsch harries the whole white army with his queen and knight. Meanwhile, the white king's rook will not run away.

| 35 | ♔d1 | ♕f1+ |
|----|-----|------|
| 36 | ♔d2 | |

Or 36 ♔c2 ♕d3+ 37 ♔b2 ♞a4 with a 'problem mate' (Nimzowitsch).

| 36 | ... | ♕d3+ |
|----|-----|------|
| 37 | ♔e1 | ♕g3+ |
| 38 | ♔f1 | ♕xh4 |

With the shelter of his king completely swept away White is hopelessly lost. Black's material investment amounts to a mere exchange and he will soon annex some more of White's pawns.

| 39 | ♔g1 | ♕g3+ |
|----|-----|------|
| 40 | ♔h1 | ♕h3+ |
| 41 | ♔g1 | ♞xe4 |
| 42 | ♕c6+ | |

Taking a circuitous route to the defence of the white king.

| 42 | ... | ♔f7 |
|----|-----|------|
| 43 | ♕c7+ | ♔g6 |
| 44 | ♕g7+ | ♔h5 |
| 45 | ♕g2 | ♕e3+ |
| 46 | ♔h2 | ♞f2 |

| 47 | ♖f1 |
|----|-----|

Or 47 ♖g1 ♕e2 and White has no checks (Nimzowitsch).

| 47 | ... | ♘g4+ |
|----|-----|------|
| 48 | ♔h1 | e4 |

The only danger Black has to avoid is an accidental stalemate. White's advance of the a-pawn is an attempt to generate this accident.

| 49 | ♖g1 | f5 |
|----|-----|-----|
| 50 | a4 | ♔xh6 |
| 51 | a5 | ♔g5 |
| 52 | ♖b1 | f3 |
| 53 | ♕b2 | f2 |
| | 0–1 | |

In spite of Nimzowitsch's impressive victory in this game, this is another line which is objectively dubious for Black. For this reason, our main chapter on 1 e4 ♘c6 2 d4, concentrates on 2...e5 as Black's major reply.

A further idea, involving a gambit, also makes surrender of the centre with 3...dxe4 seem less than attractive.

## Game 9
## Milner-Barry - Mieses
*Margate 1935*

| 1 | e4 | ♘c6 |
|---|-----|-----|
| 2 | d4 | d5 |
| 3 | ♘c3 | dxe4 |
| 4 | d5 | ♘e5 |

| 5 | f3 |
|---|-----|

An adventurous gambit alternative to 5 ♗f4. Also possible is 5 ♕d4.

| 5 | ... | exf3 |
|---|-----|------|

Black demonstrates excessive confidence in his ability to defend the resulting position. More circumspect and better would have been 5...e3, refusing the poisoned chalice.

| 6 | ♘xf3 | ♘xf3+ |
|---|------|-------|
| 7 | ♕xf3 | ♘f6 |
| 8 | ♗f4 | a6 |

The threat was now 9 ♘b5.

| 9 | h3 | g6 |
|---|-----|-----|

If 9...♗f5, then 10 ♗xc7 ♕xc7 11 ♕xf5 regains the pawn, though this could hardly have been worse than the text.

| 10 | g4 | ♗g7 |
|----|-----|-----|

**11    0-0-0**

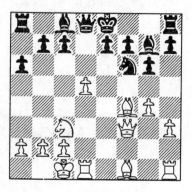

**11    ...    ♗d7**

After 11...0-0 12 ♕g3 ♘e8 13 h4 White gains a huge attack against the black king, much as in the game.

| 12 | ♕g3 | ♖c8 |
|---|---|---|
| 13 | ♗e2 | 0-0 |
| 14 | h4 | c6 |
| 15 | h5 | ♘xd5 |

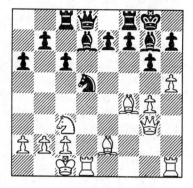

**16    hxg6**

White's attack is on the point of crashing through. Now 16...hxg6 allows 17 ♕h4 ♖e8 18 ♕h7+ ♔f8 19 ♗h6, while 16...♘xf4 17 ♕xf4 fxg6 18

♗c4+ ♔h8 19 ♖xh7+ ♔xh7 20 ♖h1+ ♗h6 21 ♕xh6 is mate. In this variation 18...e6 is a superior parry to the check but after 19 ♕e3 the threats of ♗xe6+ and ♖xd7 followed by ♗xe6 are impossible to meet.

Black's material advantage is completely irrelevant in the face of White's overpowering attack.

| 16 | ... | ♗xc3 |
|---|---|---|
| 17 | ♕h4 | ♘f6 |
| 18 | g5 | ♕a5 |
| 19 | gxf6 | h5 |

A last vain effort to check the impetus of the attack. Now White finishes off effortlessly.

| 20 | gxf7+ | ♔xf7 |
|---|---|---|
| 21 | ♗xh5+ | 1-0 |

**Section C**
**Modern Times**
The next two games show the attraction that the ideas of Nimzowitsch, Chigorin and Bogoljubow still exert over modern grandmasters.

Game 10
**Piket-Christiansen**
*Monaco Blindfold 1993*

**1    d4    ♘c6**
Starting with Bogoljubow.
**2    e4**
Avoiding the Chigorin.
**2    ...    d5**
Finally Black transposes to Nimzowitsch's Defence.

| 3 | e5 | ♗f5 |
|---|---|---|
| 4 | c3 | f6 |
| 5 | ♘f3 | |

refuge in sight for White's king.

| 5 | ... | fxe5 |

Normally Black would not release the tension so quickly, 5...♕d7 being the more orthodox move in this case.

| 6 | dxe5 |

White has an interesting gambit with 6 ♗b5! exd4 7 ♘xd4 or 6 ♗b5 e4 7 ♘e5.

| 6 | ... | e6 |
| 7 | ♗b5 |

This is a standard pin by White who is attempting to increase his control over the e5-square.

| 7 | ... | ♗c5 |
| 8 | ♘d4 | ♗xd4 |
| 9 | cxd4 | ♕h4 |

White's somewhat dilatory play has allowed Black to seize the initiative. Black's queen occupies a most threatening post.

| 10 | ♘c3 | ♘ge7 |
| 11 | ♗e3 | 0–0 |
| 12 | ♖c1 | ♗g4 |
| 13 | ♕d2 | ♘f5 |

All Black's pieces are in active play and there is no safe

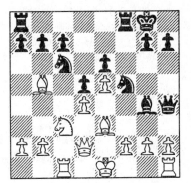

| 14 | ♗g5 | ♕h5 |
| 15 | ♗xc6 | bxc6 |
| 16 | h3 | h6 |
| 17 | ♕f4 |

This meets with an interesting refutation but, if instead 17 ♗f4 ♘h4! 18 hxg4 ♘xg2+ 19 ♔e2 ♕xg4+ then Black wins.

| 17 | ... | ♗f3!! |

A beautiful thrust which leaves White's position full of holes.

| 18 | ♕xf3 | ♕xg5 |
| 19 | 0–0 | ♘xd4 |

White has no defence and

rapidly loses several pawns.

| 20 | ♕g4 | ♕xe5 |
|----|-----|------|
| 21 | ♖ce1 | ♕f6 |
| 22 | ♘a4 | e5 |
| 23 | ♘c5 | ♕d6 |
| 24 | b4 | ♖f4 |
| 25 | ♕g3 | ♖af8 |
| 26 | ♘d3 | |

| 26 | ... | ♘f3+ |
|----|-----|------|

Elegant to the last.

| 27 | gxf3 | ♖xf3 |
|----|------|------|
| 28 | ♕xe5 | ♕g6+ |
| 29 | ♔h1 | |

29 ♔h2 ♕xd3 is equally hopeless for him.

| 29 | ... | ♖xh3+ |
|----|-----|-------|
| | **0–1** | |

A beautiful example of the dynamic counterplay and very swift imbalance Black can generate with this defence.

### Game 11
### Kasparov-Smyslov
*Vilnius Ct 1984*

| 1 | d4 | ♘c6 |
|---|-----|------|
| 2 | ♘f3 | d5 |
| 3 | c4 | ♗g4 |

| 4 | cxd5 | ♗xf3 |
|---|------|------|
| 5 | gxf3 | ♕xd5 |
| 6 | e3 | e5 |

In the main body of the text (see page 120) we prefer 6...e6 which preserves Black's second bishop.

| 7 | ♘c3 | ♗b4 |
|---|-----|------|
| 8 | ♗d2 | ♗xc3 |
| 9 | bxc3 | ♕d6 |

The whole point of playing this defence against Kasparov was to unsettle him with something unusual. In that sense this move is consistent. In the orthodox lines of the Chigorin Black normally plays 9...exd4 10 cxd4 and then ...♘ge7 or ...♘f6. The text plans to sidestep an exchange of queens based on ♕b3.

| 10 | ♖b1 | b6 |
|----|-----|-----|
| 11 | f4 | |

A radical way of clarifying the central tension.

| 11 | ... | exf4 |
|----|-----|------|
| 12 | e4 | ♘ge7 |
| 13 | ♕f3 | 0-0 |
| 14 | ♗xf4 | ♕a3 |

With the threat of ...♘xd4.

| 15 | ♗e2 | f5 |
|----|-----|-----|
| 16 | 0-0 | |

| 16 | ... | fxe4? |
|----|-----|-------|

Here Black misses the best path. According to Kasparov 16...♘g6! 17 ♗xc7 ♖ac8 18 exf5 ♖xc7 19 ♕d5+ ♔h8 20 fxg6 ♘e7 is unclear. Slightly better for White is 17 ♗c4+ ♔h8 18 ♗c1 fxe4 19 ♕xe4 ♕d6, though Black's position remains quite playable. White has the two bishops but his kingside is broken up.

| 17 | ♕xe4 | ♕xc3 |
|----|------|------|
| 18 | ♗e3 | ♕a3 |
| 19 | ♗d3 | ♕d6 |
| 20 | ♕xh7+ | ♔f7 |
| 21 | ♖b5 | ♘xd4 |
| 22 | ♕e4? | |

Faced by Smyslov's ingenious defence Kasparov misses 22 ♗xd4 ♕xd4 23 ♖g5 ♔e6 24 ♕h3+ ♔d6 25 ♗e2 ♘d5 26 ♖xd5+ which wins.

| 22 | ... | ♖ad8 |
|----|-----|------|

If 22...♘xb5 23 ♗c4+ ♔f6 24 ♕h4+ wins.

| 23 | ♗xd4 | ♕xd4 |
|----|------|------|
| 24 | ♖f5+ | |

Settling for half a point.

| 24 | ... | ♘xf5 |
|----|-----|------|
| 25 | ♕xf5+ | ♔g8 |

Not 25...♕f6 26 ♗c4+ ♔e7 27 ♖e1+ winning.

| 26 | ♕h7+ | ♔f7 |
|----|------|------|
| | ½-½ | |

It is perpetual after 27 ♕f5+.

## Section D
## Practising What We Preach

The following games are included for two reasons:

a) to demonstrate to readers that we have actually played the 1...♘c6 defence ourselves.

b) to show the beneficial effects of emulating a fine strategic example.

As a young player, I (RDK) was most impressed with the game won by Nimzowitsch in 1921 against the three consulting partners at Uppsala. In this game, Nimzowitsch castled queenside and then tore up the opposing king's fortress on the other side of the board by means of a patient pawn avalanche. Castling on the opposite sides of the board can often lead to ferocious attacks with a decisive result as the outcome. *Veneration - inspiration - emulation* was the motto!

This was my objective in choosing Nimzowitsch's Defence, namely, to unbalance the position and make it strategically difficult for both sides. Indeed, it is noticeable in several of my early games how swiftly Black either managed to castle queenside or tuck his king away safely in the centre, and then annihilate the white king by launching an attack with doubled rooks on the h-file. I think this kind of lesson, as first preached by Nimzowitsch, is most instructive for any aspiring player.

### Game 12
### Charnley-Keene
*London 1964*

| 1 | e4 | ♘c6 |
|---|-----|------|
| 2 | d4 | d5 |
| 3 | e5 | ♗f5 |
| 4 | c3 | e6 |
| 5 | ♗d3 | |

It looks sensible to challenge Black's light squared bishop, but paradoxically, it is often Black who eventually seizes control of the light squares after this exchange.

| 5 | ... | ♗xd3 |
|---|------|------|
| 6 | ♕xd3 | ♘ge7 |

| 7 | ♗g5 | |
|---|------|--|

An alternative here is 7 ♘f3 h5 8 ♘bd2 ♘f5 9 0–0 ♕d7 10 ♖e1 ♗e7 11 ♘f1 0–0–0 12 b4 f6 with a sharp position and chances for both sides as was seen in the game Pike-Keene, London 1964.

| 7 | ... | h6 |
|----|------|------|
| 8 | ♗xe7 | ♕xe7 |
| 9 | f4 | ♕d7 |
| 10 | ♘f3 | ♘e7 |
| 11 | 0–0 | h5 |

A standard precaution, preparing ...♘f5 and discouraging White from a future g4. If White does insist on playing g4 ultimately, the insertion of ...h5 helps Black to gain compensating hold on the open h-file.

| 12 | g3 | |
|----|------|--|

Not 12 h3?, when 12...h4 paralyses White's kingside pawns. With the text, White is trying to keep his kingside pawns in perfect order, hoping, one day, to achieve g4 with advantage.

| 12 | ... | ♘f5 |
| 13 | ♘bd2 | c5 |

Black plays on both wings. He maintains the choice of trading on d4 or implementing a general queenside pawn avalanche.

| 14 | ♖fc1 | ♗e7 |

Completing development and preparing to connect the rooks.

| 15 | ♘f1 | b5 |
| 16 | h3 | c4 |

Black opts for blockade.

| 17 | ♕c2 | ♕b7 |
| 18 | a3 | a5 |
| 19 | ♕d1 | ♔d7 |

The safest haven for Black's king. It is interesting in this variation how often Black delays castling, or even omits it altogether.

| 20 | g4 | |

White had to undertake something, but now the opening of the h-file plays into Black's hands. Conversely, if White did nothing, Black would simply have pressed forwards on the queen's flank, by means of ...b4.

| 20 | ... | hxg4 |
| 21 | hxg4 | ♘h4 |
| 22 | ♘g3 | ♘xf3+ |
| 23 | ♕xf3 | g6 |
| 24 | ♔g2 | b4 |

Now Black has the initiative on both wings. If White ever tries to strike back, by means of f4-f5, then Black simply trades on f5 (...gxf5) with further threats against White's exposed king.

| 25 | ♘e2 | ♖h4 |
| 26 | axb4 | ♖ah8 |

The climax of Black's attack. Black could simply have played 26...axb4, but the text sets an amusing trap.

| 27 | ♖xa5? | |

Falling head-long into the trap. White had to play the passive 27 ♖h1.

| 27 | ... | ♖h2+ |
| 28 | ♔g1 | ♖8h3 |
| 29 | ♘g3 | ♗h4 |

Black's manoeuvre has won a piece in broad daylight.

**30 ♖ca1**

This trick permits White to save his queen, but he remains a knight down with a hopeless position.

| | | |
|---|---|---|
| 30 | ... | ♖xg3+ |
| 31 | ♕xg3 | ♗xg3 |
| 32 | ♖a7 | ♔c7 |

Black emerges a piece ahead with an easy win.

| | | |
|---|---|---|
| 33 | ♖xb7+ | ♔xb7 |
| 34 | ♖f1 | ♖xb2 |
| 35 | f5 | gxf5 |
| 36 | gxf5 | ♗h4 |
| 37 | fxe6 | fxe6 |
| 38 | ♖c1 | ♗g5 |
| | 0–1 | |

Game 13
**Hindley-Keene**
*Correspondence 1963*

| | | |
|---|---|---|
| 1 | e4 | ♞c6 |
| 2 | d4 | d5 |
| 3 | e5 | ♗f5 |
| 4 | ♞e2 | e6 |
| 5 | ♞g3 | ♗g6 |
| 6 | c3 | f6 |
| 7 | f4 | ♞h6 |

It is important, when White has claimed so much of the centre with his pawns, to keep a firm grip over the blockading square f5.

| | | |
|---|---|---|
| 8 | ♞d2 | ♞f5 |
| 9 | ♞f3 | ♕d7 |
| 10 | ♗d2 | |

This development of the bishop is somewhat passive. It seems more sensible to develop White's king's bishop instead, either on e2 or b5.

| | | |
|---|---|---|
| 10 | ... | ♞ce7 |

Reinforcing the blockade of f5.

**11 ♘e2?**

This is a catastrophic retreat. White's threat of g4 is easily parried and now Black swiftly seizes the initiative.

| 11 | ... | ♗h5 |
|----|-----|-----|
| 12 | ♘g3 | ♗g4 |
| 13 | ♗d3 | ♘xg3 |
| 14 | hxg3 | ♘f5 |
| 15 | ♔f2 | |

It is a choice between this humiliating king move to defend g3 or the supine exchange 15 ♗xf5. The latter would, however, have been somewhat preferable.

| 15 | ... | 0-0-0 |
|----|-----|-------|
| 16 | ♕b3 | c5 |

Now both White's king and queen are in the firing line. It is fascinating to observe how quickly Black can obtain a winning position with this defence if White's play is hesitant.

| 17 | ♘h2 | ♘h6 |
|----|-----|-----|
| 18 | ♘xg4 | ♘xg4+ |
| 19 | ♔f3 | |

Hoping for 19...c4? 20 ♗xc4 dxc4 21 ♕xc4+ followed by ♔xg4 when the worst is over.

| 19 | ... | ♘h6 |
|----|-----|-----|
| 20 | ♕b5 | |

Now seeking relief in the exchange of queens, but Black transfers his attention to White's exposed king.

| 20 | ... | ♕f7 |
|----|-----|-----|
| 21 | c4? | |

A final blunder which loses material. It would have been better to launch a hand-to-hand fight with 21 exf6 gxf6 22 dxc5

e5 though White is severely handicapped by the presence of his king in the middle of hostilities.

| 21 | ... | fxe5 |
|----|-----|------|
| 22 | cxd5 | ♘f5 |
| 23 | dxe6 | |

This loses a piece but 23 ♗xf5 ♕xf5 was also very poor.

| 23 | ... | ♘xd4+ |
|----|-----|-------|
| 24 | ♔f2 | ♘xb5 |
| 25 | exf7 | ♖xd3 |
| 26 | ♔e2 | e4 |
| | 0-1 | |

**Game 14**
**Sandiford-Keene**
*Dulwich 1961*

| 1 | e4 | ♘c6 |
|---|-----|-----|
| 2 | d4 | d5 |
| 3 | e5 | f6 *(D)* |

Nimzowitsch's original idea, which is far more challenging than 3...♗f5.

| 4 | f4 | ♗f5 |
|---|-----|-----|
| 5 | ♘e2 | ♕d7 |
| 6 | ♘g3 | ♗g4 |
| 7 | ♗e2 | ♗xe2 |

As so often in this defence, the trade of light-squared bishops furthers Black's aims rather than White's.

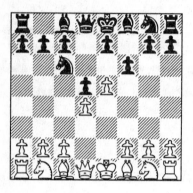

| 8 | ♘xe2 | e6 |
| 9 | ♗e3 | ♘ge7 |

Almost imperceptibly, Black has gained tangible influence over the centre and White's remaining dark-squared bishop is seriously restricted by its own pawns.

| 10 | 0-0 | ♘f5 |
| 11 | ♕d2 | h5 |

Once again, this strategically valuable advance of Black's h-pawn plays a vital role.

| 12 | ♘g3 | |

A common factor in this opening is that White simply cannot stand the presence of the black knight on f5 and therefore accepts doubled pawns in order to eliminate it. However, White's doubled pawns on the g-file represent an attractive target for Black's further attack, by means of ...h4.

| 12 | ... | ♘xg3 |

| 13 | hxg3 | ♘e7 |
| 14 | ♗f2 | f5 |

Black no longer requires the f5-square for his knight. It is more important to fix White's pawn on g3 as a weakness in preparation for the line-opening attack ...h4.

| 15 | ♘a3 | ♘g6 |
| 16 | ♕d3 | ♔f7 |

A vital step in connecting Black's rooks. The king is safer on f7 than it would be after ...0-0-0.

| 17 | c4 | ♗xa3 |
| 18 | ♕xa3 | h4 |

The final attack commences. There is no need to risk the opening of the position after 18...dxc4.

| 19 | cxd5 | ♕xd5 |
| 20 | ♖ac1 | c6 |
| 21 | ♖c5 | ♕d7 |
| 22 | b4 | h3 |

White's demonstration on the other wing comes too late. There is really no defence to Black's numerous options on the h-file.

from 1921, referred to in the introduction to this section: 6...♗xb1 7 ♖xb1 0-0-0 8 cxd5 ♕xd5 9 ♗xc6 ♕xc6 10 0-0 e6 11 ♗e3 ♘e7 12 ♕e2 ♘d5 13 ♖fc1 ♕d7 14 ♖c4 ♔b8 15 ♕d2 ♖c8 16 ♘e1 ♗e7 17 ♘d3 ♖hd8 18 ♕c2 f5 19 ♖c1 g5 20 ♘c5 ♗xc5 21 ♖xc5 ♖g8 22 ♕e2 h5

| 23 | gxh3 | ♖xh3 |
| 24 | ♕c1 | ♖ah8 |
| 25 | b5 | ♘e7 |
| 26 | ♔g2 | b6! |

An elegant move which gains control of the vital d5-square for Black's queen.

| 27 | bxc6 | ♘xc6 |
| | **0-1** | |

28 ♖xc6 ♕d5 is checkmate, while after 28 ♖b5 ♘e7 White also loses control of the long light-squared diagonal. The next game follows an identical thematic trend.

### Game 15
### Sugden-Keene
*Dulwich 1961*

| 1 | e4 | ♘c6 |
| 2 | d4 | d5 |
| 3 | e5 | f6 |
| 4 | ♘f3 | ♗f5 |
| 5 | ♗b5 | ♕d7 |
| 6 | 0-0 | |

Varying from 6 c4, which was played in the famous Nimzowitsch consultation game

offering a sacrifice to help open lines against White's king. Indeed, Black's pawn avalanche soon broke through in decisive fashion, Three Swedish Amateurs-Nimzowitsch, Uppsala 1921.

| 6 | ... | 0-0-0 |

Already the battle lines are set. Opposite castling will lead to a very sharp fight.

| 7 | ♘c3 | e6 |
| 8 | ♗e3 | a6 (D) |
| 9 | ♗xc6 | |

This is a strategic blunder. White should either play 9 ♗e2 preserving his light-squared bishop or even 9 ♗a4 when Black would hardly consider permitting the sacrifice 9...b5

10 ♘xb5.

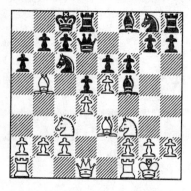

Black's pieces out of play, but weaknesses arise in its wake.

| | | |
|---|---|---|
| **13** | **g4** | **♘h6** |

Not 13...♖h3 14 ♖f3 fxg4 15 ♖xh3 gxh3 16 ♕g4 regaining control with a good position. .

| | | |
|---|---|---|
| **14** | **h3** | **♗e7** |
| **15** | **♖f2** | **♘f7** |
| **16** | **♕f3** | **♖h4** |
| **17** | **gxf5** | **gxf5** |
| **18** | **♖h2** | **♖dh8** |

| | | |
|---|---|---|
| **9** | **...** | **♕xc6** |
| **10** | **♘h4** | **♗g6** |
| **11** | **♘xg6** | **hxg6** |
| **12** | **f4** | **f5** |

Black's attack plays itself. The move ...g5 will soon smash White's position.

| | | |
|---|---|---|
| **19** | **♔h1** | **g5** |
| **20** | **♗f2** | **g4** |

This advance forces a decisive gain of material.

| | | |
|---|---|---|
| **21** | **♕e3** | **♖xh3** |
| **22** | **♗g3** | **♖xh2+** |
| **23** | **♗xh2** | **♖h3** |
| | **0-1** | |

There is no defence to ...g3.

Black already has an excellent position. He owns the half-open h-file and has a potential attack against White's king; ...g5 perhaps combined with ...♘h6-g4. Meanwhile, as so often occurs, White's remaining dark-squared bishop is an extremely feeble piece. White's next move is an ambitious attempt to gain space and lock

Game 16
**Tisdall-Jacobs**
*Gausdal 1996*

| | | |
|---|---|---|
| **1** | **d4** | **♘c6** |

**2 d5**

An earlier game of mine (BJ) from the same tournament, against the Russian grandmaster A. Ivanov, saw 2 ♘f3 d5 3 g3 ♗f5 (3...♗g4 is a perfectly playable alternative and is perhaps more dynamic - see page 131) 4 ♗g2 e6 5 0-0 ♘f6 6 ♘bd2 ♗e7 7 a3 ♘e4 8 c4 0-0 9 b3 ♗f6 (the tactical try 9...♘c3 10 ♕e1 dxc4 11 ♘xc4 ♘xd4? backfires after 12 ♘xd4 ♕xd4 13 ♗b2 ♗f6 14 ♖c1 and White wins a piece) 10 ♗b2 a5 11 ♖c1 ♕d7 12 e3 ♖fd8 13 ♕e2 and White had a small advantage.

**2 ... ♘e5**
**3 e4 e6**
**4 ♕d4**

White hopes to gain time by kicking the black knight around. However, as with Alekhine's Defence, White can find that his own position has become over-extended if he is not careful. In this game White has some difficulties with the exposed position of his queen.

The tempting alternative 4 f4 gains time and space but, again, as we have seen, White must be very wary of playing too many pawn moves while his development lags.

**4 ... ♘g6**
**5 ♘f3 ♘f6**
**6 ♘c3**

**6 ... ♗e7**

I spent a long time on this move convincing myself that Black's position was okay after White's reply. A strange-looking alternative which tries to make use of the unusual position of White's queen is 6...b6!? when play can continue 7 dxe6 (this is a critical attempt to disrupt Black's position by attacking his knight; if White continues quietly Black should not have problems, e.g. 7 ♗g5 ♗c5 8 ♕d2 h6 9 ♗xf6 ♕xf6 is fine for Black) 7...fxe6 8 e5 ♗c5 and now 9 ♕c4, preventing the knight from coming to d5 with the following possibilities:

a) 9...♘g8 might be playable but White has dangerous tries such as 10 ♗g5 ♘xe5 11 ♕e4 ♘xf3+ 12 ♕xf3 ♕xg5 13 ♕xa8 ♘e7 14 ♘e4 ♕e5 15 0-0-0 0-0 16 ♘xc5 ♕xc5; 10 h4 ♗b7 11 ♗g5 ♘8e7 12 h5 ♘f8 13 ♘e4; or finally, 10 b4 ♗e7 11 ♘b5 c6 12 ♘d6+ ♗xd6 13 exd6.

b) 9...d5 fails to the accurate continuation 10 ♕a4+! ♗d7 (10...♘d7 11 ♕c6) 11 ♗b5 and Black is in trouble, e.g. 11...a6 12 ♗xd7+ ♘xd7 13 ♕c6 and the e-pawn cannot be sensibly defended.

**7 h4 h5**

Wilhelm Steinitz, who was well-known for his love of constricted positions, would probably have rejoiced in Black's position after 7...0-0 8 h5 ♘h8, but I didn't like the look of it.

**8 ♗g5 0-0**

It looks as though Black's h-pawn must be terribly weak but, as the game progresses, it becomes clear that this is not the whole story and that White's

weakness on g4 is also a very important feature of the position.

**9 0-0-0 d6**

Black is planning to close the centre with ...e5 and White decides to prevent this.

**10 dxe6 ♗xe6**
**11 ♘d5**

This move allows Black to force a favourable simplification. White would have done better to maintain the tension with a simple developing move such as 11 ♗c4.

**11 ... ♗xd5**
**12 exd5 ♘g4**

From now until the end of the game White's f-pawn proves to be an annoying weakness for him.

**13 ♗d3 ♗f6**
**14 ♗xf6 ♕xf6**
**15 ♕xf6 gxf6**

The slight weakness of Black's kingside pawn structure is compensated for by the active positioning of his knights.

**16 ♖d2 ♘f4**
**17 ♗f5 ♖ae8**
**18 ♖e1**

18 g3 appears to tidy up the white position but then the black knights come into their own, e.g. 18...♘e2+ 19 ♔b1 ♘xf2 20 ♖h2 (or 20 ♖e1 ♘xg3 21 ♖g1 ♘fh1! when Black's knights are on very strange squares but it is not at all clear that White can exploit this) 20...♘g1! and the weakness of White's back rank means that

Black will escape with an extra pawn.

| | | |
|---|---|---|
| 18 | ... | ♖xe1+ |
| 19 | ♞xe1 | ♖e8 |

| | | |
|---|---|---|
| 20 | ♔d1 | ½-½ |

The position is equal. Black's active knights fully compensate for the weakened pawns.

This game demonstrated a typical by-product of playing ...♞c6 - Tisdall used up nearly an hour on his first six moves, including 20 minutes on 2 d5. His comment on the opening after the game was: 'It looked terrible for Black but, actually, it's not at all bad'.

The moral to be drawn from this is that the white player runs terrible dangers if he underestimates Black's resources.

# 2    1 e4 ♘c6 2 d4 e5

| 1 | e4 | ♘c6 |
|---|-----|-----|
| 2 | d4  | e5  |

With this move, Black launches a swift central attack on the dark squares and immediately gives White a problem with the threat to his d-pawn. There are three ways that White can counter this early attack and the manner of response lays the foundation for the ensuing middlegame.

## i) Capturing with 3 dxe5
By playing like this, White hopes that Black's central knight will provide a target and help him to develop his pieces. White can attack this knight with moves such as ♘f3, ♗f4 or, most adventurously, f4.

Black, for his part, will try to maintain the knight on e5 and by doing so keep control of the central dark squares. If he is obliged to exchange this piece, he will be looking to simplify the position with further exchanges. An important theme for Black in this variation is the move ...♗b4+ which can often prove awkward for White. For example, if White drives the bishop away with c3, then he has taken the natural development square away from his queen's knight. Alternatively, he could try ♗d2, but then there is a danger that Black will exchange pieces and the position will become too simplified for White to hope for an advantage.

## ii) Advancing with 3 d5
White gains space in the centre as well as some time by driving the black knight back. If White now continues (after 3...♘ce7) 4 c4, we have a direct transposition into the lines which more commonly arise from the sequence 1 d4 ♘c6 2 c4 e5 3 d5 ♘ce7 4 e4, considered in chapter five. Here we consider attempts by White to avoid c4.

This plan should not be troublesome for Black as he has a very flexible position and can develop in King's Indian fashion with ...g6 and ...f5 or play more adventurously by developing the bishop on a more active square such as b4 or c5.

### iii) 3 ♘f3 - The Scotch Game

By playing 3 ♘f3, White transposes directly to the Scotch Game. This is an important option for White and so here we consider defences for Black against the two most popular ways of playing the Scotch for White.

### Game 17
### Gi. Garcia-Miles
*Linares 1994*

| 1 | e4 | ♘c6 |
|---|-----|------|
| 2 | d4 | e5 |
| 3 | dxe5 | ♘xe5 |
| 4 | ♘f3 | ♗b4+ |
| 5 | c3 | ♘xf3+ |
| 6 | ♕xf3 | ♗c5 |

**7   b4!?**

An adventurous try from White, trying to take the initiative at a very early stage. White hopes to gain time and space by this advance but the drawback is that his position could become over-extended. Others:

a) 7 ♗c4 is a simple alternative which incidentally threatens mate. Solomon-Miles, Melbourne 1991 continued 7...♕f6 8 ♗f4 d6 9 ♘d2 ♘e7 10 0-0-0 (this, combined with White's next move, constitutes an ambitious plan, but he is unlikely to get anywhere with the quiet 10 0-0) 10...0-0 11 h4 ♘c6 (11...♘g6 immediately should also be fine, although White would then have more options - e.g. 12 ♗g3 or 12 g3 - than he does in the game) 12 ♕g3 ♘e5 13 ♗e2 ♘g6 14 ♗e3 ♗xe3 15 ♕xe3 ♕f4 (Black has a slight initiative) 16 ♘f1 ♖e8 17 ♕xf4 ♘xf4 18 ♗f3 ♗e6 19 b3 a5 20 ♘e3 a4 and Black's chances are preferable.

b) With 7 ♗d3 White leaves the c4-square free as he has a plan in mind to harry the black bishop, e.g. 7...d6 8 ♘d2 ♘e7 9 b4 ♗b6 10 ♘c4 0-0 11 0-0 ♗e6 12 a4 (White continues with his plan, but his queenside structure is quickly becoming exposed and this soon tells against him) 12...c6 13 ♘xb6 axb6 14 ♕e2 ♗b3 15 ♗c2 ♗xc2 16 ♕xc2 b5 17 ♗e3 bxa4 18 ♖xa4 ♖xa4 19 ♕xa4 ♕d7 20 ♖d1 ♕e6 21 ♕c2 d5 (Black has completely equalised) 22 ♗c5 (White should have reconciled himself to 22 exd5 as the text backfires on account of White's weak back rank) 22...dxe4 23 ♖d6 ♖a8 24 h3 ♕e5 25 ♕a2 (White tries a back-rank trick of his own, but the damage has already been done) 25...♖e8 26 ♖d7 ♘d5 27 ♗d4 ♕b8 28 ♕e2 ♕c8 29 ♕g4 g6 30 c4 h5 31 ♕g5 ♕xd7 32 ♕h6 ♘f6 0-1 B. Martin-Miles, Auckland 1992.

c) 7 ♗e3 is rather insipid. After 7...♗xe3 8 ♕xe3 ♘f6 9 ♘d2 0-0 10 ♗d3 ♖e8 11 0-0 d5 12 ♖ae1 ♗f5 13 ♕f3 dxe4 14 ♘xe4 ♗xe4 15 ♗xe4 Black was completely equal in Thipsay-Miles, Calcutta Open 1994.

**7 ... ♗b6**

An alternative scheme of development is 7...♗e7 8 ♗c4 ♗f6 eyeing the slight weakness on c3.

**8 ♘d2 ♘e7**

**9 a4**

White must be careful not to

waste too much time, due his slightly undeveloped state. For example 9 ♘c4 0-0 10 a4 comes unstuck after the instructive reply 10...d5! 11 exd5 ♘xd5 and if now 12 a5? ♖e8+ 13 ♗e2 ♘xc3! Black wins, as ...♗d4 follows if White captures the knight.

**9 ... c6!?**

Black is trying to provoke White into over-extending himself - a common theme in this variation. For the less adventurously inclined, the simple 9...a6 was a perfectly sound alternative. The play now assumes a forcing nature.

**10 ♘c4 ♗c7**
**11 e5!**

White must continue his strategy aggressively, otherwise his position will become exposed to a quick black counter-attack. For example after 11 ♗f4 d5 Black already stands well.

**11 ... 0-0**

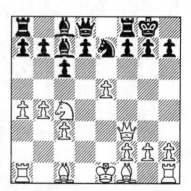

**12 ♗g5**

Again it is essential for White to continue actively as Black, although cramped, is poised to take the initiative with moves such as ...♘g6 or ...f6 when White will regret his lack of development.

**12    ...        ♛e8**

Black side-steps the pin and threatens to bring intolerable pressure to bear on the white e-pawn with ...♘g6. White's continuation is thus forced.

**13    ♘d6       ♗xd6**
**14    exd6      ♘d5+!**

This is much stronger than the attempt to round up the White e-pawn. After 14...♘f5+ the logical conclusion of the game may well be a curious draw, i.e. 15 ♚d2! ♛e6 (not 15...♘xd6 16 ♖e1 when the black queen is 'checkmated') 16 ♗d3 ♘xd6 17 ♖he1 ♘c4+ 18 ♚c2 (not 18 ♚d1 ♛d6 and Black threatens ...♘e5, ...♘b2+ and possibly ...♛xd3+ as well) 18...♘a3+! (18...♘e5 19 ♛h5 g6 20 ♛h4 is extremely dangerous for Black) 19 ♚b2 ♘c4+ with perpetual check.

**15    ♚d2**

15 ♗e2 saves White the inconvenience of having to move his king, but leaves him stuck for a decent reply after 15...♛e5! striking all his weak points.

**15    ...        ♛e6**

15...♛e5 looks tempting but White has a satisfactory reply with 16 ♛g3!.

**16    ♛g3       f6**
**17    ♗h6       ♛f7**

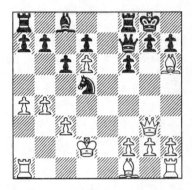

**18    ♗c4**

Miles points out the amusing variation 18 ♗e2 ♚h8! 19 ♗h5? ♛g8! (Black defends in true Steinitzian fashion) 20 ♗f4 ♘xf4 and ...♛d5+ will pick up a piece.

**18    ...        ♚h8!**
**19    ♗f4       b5!**

White has been making all the running but has not succeeded in inflicting serious weaknesses on the black position. Now Miles bursts out to exploit the exposed white queenside and the highly insecure position of his king.

**20  ♗b3**

White can accept Black's gambit with 20 axb5 cxb5 21 ♗xb5 but after 21...♗b7 Black has excellent compensation. Not many players would be attracted to this white position with the king wandering around in midboard.

| 20 | ... | ♗b7 |
|----|-----|-----|
| 21 | ♕f3 | c5! |

Opening further lines towards the white king and incidentally gaining time thanks to the threat of ...♘xf4.

| 22 | ♗g3 | cxb4 |
|----|-----|------|
| 23 | cxb4 | bxa4 |
| 24 | ♖xa4 | ♘b6! |
| 25 | ♕d3 | |

25 ♗xf7 ♗xf3 26 ♖a2 ♗xg2 wins for Black.

| 25 | ... | ♕h5! |

![chess diagram]

The contrast with the position of just a few moves ago is remarkable. The black forces have emerged from confine-

ment and are now roaming the board freely. White has so many exposed points that it is only a matter of time before he has an accident.

| 26 | ♖a5 | ♕g4 |
|----|-----|-----|
| 27 | f4 | f5! |

When you have a good position it is often wise to continue improving it rather than grabbing material. Here Black is in no hurry to capture on g2, which might give White time to co-ordinate his forces, and instead fixes a further weakness on f4, locks the white dark-squared bishop out of the game and prepares to bring his rook to f6, menacing the white d-pawn.

| 28 | ♖e1 | ♕g6 |
|----|-----|-----|
| 29 | ♕d4 | ♖f6 |
| 30 | ♖ae5 | ♖af8 |

The white d-pawn is now indefensible.

| 31 | ♔c1 | ♖xd6 |
|----|-----|------|
| 32 | ♕c3 | ♗d5 |

Black continues methodically, exchanging off White's better minor piece and further

exposing his king. White could
safely resign here.

|    |        |         |
|----|--------|---------|
| 33 | ♔b1    | ♖c6     |
| 34 | ♕e3    | ♕f7     |
| 35 | ♖e8    | ♖c8     |
| 36 | ♖xf8+  | ♖xf8    |
| 37 | ♔b2    | h6      |
| 38 | ♗f2    | ♖c8     |
| 39 | ♗xd5   | ♕xd5    |
| 40 | ♕d4    | ♕c6     |

**41    ♕c5**

A blunder, but White's position was hopeless.

**0-1**

41...♘a4+ picks up the white
queen.

### Game 18
### **Kudrin-Miles**
*US Championship 1989*

|   |       |            |
|---|-------|------------|
| 1 | e4    | ♘c6        |
| 2 | d4    | e5         |
| 3 | dxe5  | ♘xe5       |
| 4 | ♘f3   | ♗b4+*(D)*  |
| 5 | c3    |            |

White can also consider other
ways of blocking the bishop
check:

a) 5 ♗d2 leads to an immediate simplification of the position which should leave Black
without serious difficulties, e.g.
5...♗xd2+ 6 ♘bxd2 ♕f6 7
♘xe5 ♕xe5 8 c3 ♘e7 9 ♗d3
0-0 10 0-0 ♘g6 11 ♖e1 d6
(Black has an easy game) 12
♗f1 ♗d7 13 ♘c4 ♕g5 14 ♕d2
♕xd2 15 ♘xd2 ♖fe8 16 g3 ♗c6
17 ♗g2 ♘e5 18 ♖ab1 ♖e7 19
f4 ♘d7 20 ♖e3 ♖ae8 21 ♖be1
f5 22 h3 ♔f8 23 ♔f2 ♘c5 24 e5
dxe5 25 ♗xc6 bxc6 26 fxe5
♖xe5 and Black went on to win
in Zaninotto-Miles, Mendrisio
1989.

b) 5 ♘c3 is untested but a
logical continuation for Black is
5...♘xf3+ 6 ♕xf3 ♕f6 which
looks equal as 7 ♕g3 can be
comfortably met by 7...♕g6

c) 5 ♘bd2 is the most dy-
namic of White's alternatives,
e.g. 5...♘xf3+ 6 ♕xf3 ♘e7
(6...♕f6 followed by ...♘e7 is
another scheme of development) 7 a3 ♗a5 8 b4 ♗b6 9
♗b2 0-0 10 ♗c4 (10 ♕g3 f6

and Black is preparing to hit back in the centre with ...d5.) 10...♘c6 11 ♘b3 White is now threatening ♕g3 - on the previous move this would have been met by ...♗d4 - which would cause a serious weakness in the black kingside) 11...♕h4 12 g3 (White is trying to create an initiative on the kingside, but this weakness has long-term repercussions) 12...♕h6 13 ♖d1 d6 (due to the weakness created by g3, it is now impossible for the white king to find a secure home) 14 ♖d5? ♗e6 15 ♖h5 ♕g6 16 ♗e2 f5! 17 exf5 ♗xf5 18 0-0 ♖ae8 (Black has smoothly completed his development while White has been driven back in confusion) 19 ♗d1 ♗e4 20 ♕c3 ♘e5 21 ♘d4

21...♗xd4! 22 ♕xd4 ♗f3 (White's over-ambitious plan of switching his rook to h5 has backfired and it now provides a target for Black) 23 ♖xe5 (23 ♖h3 ♕f5 leaves White without a sensible reply) 23...dxe5 24 ♕c3 ♗xd1 25 ♖xd1 ♕f7 26 ♕e3 ♕f3 and Black won easily, Gi. Garcia-Miles, Matanzas Capablanca Memorial 1995.

**5 ... ♗d6!?**

This is an imaginative alternative to the straightforward capture on f3.

**6 ♘bd2**

Or 6 ♘xe5 ♗xe5 7 f4 ♗d6 8 ♗e3 ♕e7 9 ♕f3 ♗c5 10 ♗c4 ♗xe3 11 ♕xe3 (White seems to be making all the running but Black now finds a neat equalising blow) 11...d5 12 ♗xd5 ♘f6 13 ♗b3 ♕xe4 14 ♕xe4+ ♘xe4 15 0-0 0-0 16 ♖e1 ♘c5 17 ♗c2 ♗e6 18 b4 ♘d7 19 f5 ♗d5 20 ♘a3 ♘f6 21 c4 ♗c6 22 b5 ♗d7 23 h3 h5 24 ♔f2 ♖fe8 and Black drew without difficulty, Popovych-Emms, London Lloyds Bank 1990.

**6 ... ♘xf3+**
**7 ♘xf3 ♘e7**
**8 e5**

Black's defence has reacted on the white player like a red rag to a bull and he now proceeds to charge at his opponent without any thought for the safety of his own pawn structure.

| 8 | ... | ♗c5 |

**9 b4?!**

One of the attractive features of this variation for Black is that White often overstretches himself while searching for an advantage. The black position looks underdeveloped and this often encourages aggressive white players to force the play more than is justified by the situation on the board. Black's position is very solid and is unlikely to be broken down by brute force.

| 9 | ... | ♗b6 |
| 10 | ♗f4 | 0-0 |
| 11 | ♗c4 | ♘g6 |
| 12 | ♗g3 | d6! |

Suddenly Black has completed development and the early white advance with 9 b4 has just led to a weakening of the c3-square.

| 13 | exd6 |

White continues to play is if he stands well, but a more prudent course would have been 13 0-0 with equality.

| 13 | ... | ♖e8+ |
| 14 | ♗e2 | ♕f6! |

This counterattack against c3 ensures that Black regains his material.

| 15 | 0-0 | cxd6 |
| 16 | ♗b5 | |

16 ♗xd6? ♖xe2.

| 16 | ... | ♖d8 |
| 17 | ♕d2 | ♗g4 |
| 18 | ♘d4 | ♖ac8 |
| 19 | ♖ac1 | |

The weakness of the c3-pawn forces White into this passive rook placement.

| 19 | ... | ♘e5 |

The relative weaknesses appear to cancel each other out, but if anyone stands better, it is Black. As well as eyeing White's weak pawn on c3 (somewhat counterbalanced by Black's isolated pawn on the d-file), Black also has designs on occupying c4 with his knight. If now, for example, 20 c4 to fight against that weakness, then 20...♗xd4 21 ♕xd4 ♘f3+ wins White's queen.

| | | |
|---|---|---|
| 20 | ♖fe1 | ♖c7 |
| 21 | ♗f1 | a6 |
| 22 | ♖e4 | ♕g6 |
| 23 | ♖ce1 | f6 |

The weaknesses on c3 and d6 cancel each other out and so the position is complex but balanced.

**24   ♔h1   ♖dc8**

Having reinforced his central knight, Black now gradually increases the pressure against White's c-pawn.

**25   ♖4e3   ♗d7**

Black envisions a regrouping of his pieces with the knight coming to g4 and the bishop to c6.

**26   a4   h5**

Of course not 26...♗xa4 27 ♕a2+. The text combines play on both sides of the board.

| | | |
|---|---|---|
| 27 | f4 | ♘g4 |
| 28 | ♖e7 | h4 |

A neat sacrifice which allows

Black's pieces to converge on White's king from all sides.

**29   ♗xh4   ♕h5**

**30   ♗g3?**

White blunders in a complicated position. Correct was 30 ♘f3 ♕xh4 which should lead to a draw, e.g.:

a) 31 ♕a2+ ♔h8 32 ♘xh4 ♘f2+ and White would be advised to acquiesce in a draw by perpetual as 33 ♕xf2 ♗xf2 34 ♘g6+ ♔h7 35 ♖1e2 ♗a7 leaves Black with the better chances.

b) 31 ♗c4+ ♔h8 (not 31...♔h7 32 ♕c2+ or 31...♖xc4 32 ♕d5+ ♔h8 33 ♘xh4 winning) 32 ♘xh4 ♘f2+ 33 ♕xf2 (33 ♔g1 ♘e4+ 34 ♕e3 ♗xe3+ 35 ♖xe3 ♖xc4 and Black is holding the balance as 36 ♖xd7 can be met by the clever 36...♖xb4) 33...♗xf2 34 ♘g6+ ♔h7 35 ♖1e2 ♗xg6 and Black stands well.

c) 31 ♘xh4 ♘f2+ 32 ♔g1 and now Black can draw with 32...♘h3+. Trying for more with 32...♘e4+ 33 ♕e3 ♗xe3+

34 ♖xe3 d5 is dangerous after 35 c4.

**30 ... ♖xc3!**

After this blow, which White must have underestimated, the black attack assumes decisive proportions.

**31 ♖xd7 ♖xg3**
**32 h3 ♕d5!**

The immediate point is that 32 hxg4 fails to 32...♖h3+ 34 ♔g1 ♗xd4+. However, White believes that he has seen a flaw in Black's plan.

**33 ♘f3**

**33 ... ♕xf3!**

This is a neat concluding tactic from Miles. White's next is forced in order to cover the g1-square, as 31 gxf3 ♖g1 is checkmate.

**34 ♗c4+**

Vacating the back rank with tempo. White sacrifices his bishop to defend g1.

**34 ... ♖xc4**
**35 gxf3 ♖xh3+**
**36 ♔g2 ♖h2+**

The point. Black regains the queen with two extra pieces. His last remaining task is to assuage White's fury, as he doubles his rooks on the 7th rank.

**37 ♔g3 ♖xd2**

**38 ♖ee7**

White is desperately trying for a trick based on his doubled rooks on the seventh rank. This is a forlorn hope but 38 ♔xg4 ♖c7 is also completely prospectless.

**38 ... ♘h6**
**39 ♖xg7+ ♔f8**
**40 ♖h7 ♖cc2**
**41 ♖h8+ ♘g8**
**42 ♔g4 ♖g2+**
**43 ♔f5 ♖g7**
**44 ♖xd6 ♖c6**
**0-1**

A brilliant game, again revealing the hitherto undiscovered energy inherent in the unusual positions that develop from this uncharted variation.

The plan with ...e5 is not a modern invention, as the following game shows.

Game 19
**Tarve-Keres**
*Tallinn 1969*

| 1 | e4 | ♘c6 |
|---|-----|------|
| 2 | d4 | e5 |
| 3 | dxe5 | ♘xe5 |
| 4 | ♘f3 | ♕f6 |
| 5 | ♗e2 | |

After 5 ♘xe5 ♕xe5 the position has become slightly simplified but Black must be careful that his queen does not provide too much of a target for the white pieces. Play can continue 6 ♗d3 and now:

a) 6...♗c5 7 ♕e2 d6 8 ♘c3 ♘f6 9 ♗d2 ♘g4 led to complex play in Planinc-Lutikov, Skopje 1969: 10 f4 ♕e7 11 0-0-0 ♘f2 12 ♘d5 ♕d8 13 ♖df1 ♘xh1 14 ♗c3 ♔f8 (this is a strange move but if 14...0-0, then 15 ♕h5 yields what looks like a dangerous attack) 15 f5 c6 16 f6 g6 17 ♘e7 ♘f2 18 ♖xf2 ♗xf2 19 ♕xf2 ♗e6 and White proved to

have insufficient compensation for the material sacrificed, Planinc-Lutikov, Skopje 1969.

b) 6...♗b4+ 7 ♘d2 ♘f6 8 0-0 d6 9 ♘c4 ♕e7 10 c3 ♗c5 11 b4 ♗b6 12 a4 (this time Planinc has developed much more smoothly and Black has trouble co-ordinating his forces) 12...♗g4 13 ♕e1 c6 14 ♗g5 h6 15 ♗h4 ♗c7 16 f4 g5 (a rather desperate measure, but the threat of e5 was hard to counter) 17 fxg5 hxg5 18 ♗xg5 d5 19 exd5 ♗xh2+ 20 ♔f2 (White's pressure on the e- and f-files is so great that the disturbance of his king does not prove to be a problem) 20...♗e6

21 ♔e2 (it is highly unusual for a king to walk directly into the path of a discovered check but once it relocates to the queen's wing the pin against f6 will be decisive) 21...♗f5+ 22 ♔d1 ♗xd3 23 ♗xf6 ♕xe1+ 24 ♖xe1+ ♔f8 25 ♗xh8 ♗xc4 26 ♖h1 ♗b3+ 27 ♔c1 ♗d6 28 ♗f6 ♔e8 29 ♖h8+ ♗f8 30 ♗g7 1-0

Planinc-Lutikov, Skopje 1969.

| 5 | ... | ♗b4+ |

The bishop check is often awkward for White in this variation. If he meets it by interposing a piece, there is a danger that his development will not flow smoothly or that the position will become simplified. However, if he counters with c3, as here, then the natural development square for his queen's knight is taken away.

| 6 | c3 | ♗c5 |
| 7 | 0-0 | ♘e7 |
| 8 | ♘bd2 | d6 |
| 9 | ♘b3 | ♗b6 |
| 10 | ♔h1 | |

White is hoping to develop play by continuing with an exchange of knight on e5 and then f4 to generate pressure on the f-file. However, Black's next move cuts across this plan.

| 10 | ... | ♘xf3 |
| 11 | ♗xf3 | 0-0 |

Black has developed his pieces comfortably and has no problems. Meanwhile White is struggling to find anything constructive to do with his queen's bishop and, in attempting to activate this piece, he runs into difficulties.

| 12 | ♘d4 | ♘g6 |
| 13 | ♗e3 | |

White could prevent any incursions by the black knight with 13 g3 but then 13...♗h3 14 ♗g2 ♗xg2+ 15 ♔xg2 ♖fe8 leaves Black with a very pleasant position as the white kingside has been weakened and his e-pawn is exposed.

| 13 | ... | ♘h4 |
| 14 | ♘c2 | ♘xf3 |
| 15 | ♕xf3 | ♕xf3 |
| 16 | gxf3 | |

White got himself very tangled up from the opening and has tried to solve his problems by baling out into an endgame. However, the black initiative persists despite the simplified nature of the position.

| 16 | ... | f5 |
| 17 | ♔g2 | ♗d7 |
| 18 | ♗xb6 | |

Every time White exchanges pieces he is helping Black to improve his position. Here he opens the a-file for the black rook to come into the game. It was better to sit tight with 18 ♖fe1.

**18 ... axb6**
**19 ♘e3 ♖a5!**

This is very instructive play. Keres maximises the activity of his rook by keeping an eye on the white a-pawn while simultaneously threatening to switch to the kingside. In contrast 19...♖ae8 20 exf5 ♗xf5 21 ♘xf5 ♖xf5 22 ♖fe1 simplifies the position and leaves White with fewer problems to solve.

**20 ♘d5**

This works out badly, but White's position was already very difficult, e.g. 20 a3 fxe4 21 fxe4 ♖g5+ 22 ♔h1 ♖b5 and Black wins due to the dual threats of ...♗h3 and ...♖xb2; 20 exf5 ♗xf5 21 ♖fe1 (White should perhaps reconcile himself to 21 ♘xf5 ♖axf5 although

Black should then win with his extra pawn) 21...♗e6 and White cannot cope with all the threats.

**20 ... fxe4**
**21 fxe4 c6**
**22 b4**

22 ♘xb6 ♖g5+ 23 ♔h1 ♗h3 24 ♖g1 ♖h5 and the white f-pawn goes.

**22 ... ♖a3**
**23 ♘xb6**

The white knight cannot now retreat from the enemy camp but if instead 23 ♘e3 ♖xc3 he is a pawn down for nothing.

**23 ... ♗e6**

**24 f4**

One of White's problems is that 24 c4, trying to secure the knight with c5, runs into 24...♗h3+. If White tries to improve on this variation with 24 ♖fd1 then, amongst others, Black can play 24...♖xc3 25 ♖xd6 ♗h3+ 26 ♔g1 ♖f4 and, despite his extra pawn, White is unlikely to be able to beat off the rampant black pieces.

**24 ... ♖a6**

White is now losing his advanced knight.

| 25 | f5 | ♗f7 |
|----|-----|------|
| 26 | ♖fd1 | ♖d8 |
| 27 | ♘c8 | ♖xc8 |
| 28 | ♖xd6 | ♖e8 |
| 29 | ♔f3 | ♖a3 |
| | **0-1** | |

### Game 20
### Hebden-Jadoul
*Tårnby 1987*

| 1 | e4 | ♘c6 |
|----|-----|------|
| 2 | d4 | e5 |
| 3 | dxe5 | ♘xe5 |
| 4 | ♘f3 | |

4 f4 is a more aggressive way for White to handle the position. Black can then try:

a) 4...♘c6 envisages an eventual follow-up of ...♗c5 (or ...♗b4-a5-b6) to exploit the weak dark squares. Possible now are:

a1) 5 ♗e3 g6 6 ♘c3 ♗g7 7 ♕d2 ♘f6 8 ♘f3 0-0 9 0-0-0 (White could try 9 e5 ♘e8 but then Black is poised to strike

back with ...d6) 9...d6 10 h3 ♖e8 11 ♗d3 was seen in Pop-chev-Cvetkovic, Vrbas 1993. Now 11...♘b4 is equal according to Cvetkovic.

a2) 5 ♗c4 ♗b4+ (not 5...♗c5? in view of then 6 ♗xf7+) 6 c3 ♗a5 7 ♘f3 ♕e7 8 ♕e2 ♗b6 9 ♘bd2 d6 10 ♗d3 ♘f6 11 ♘c4 0-0 12 ♘xb6 axb6 13 0-0 ♖e8 14 ♖e1 h6 gave Black a solid position in the game Knaak-Przewoznik, Dortmund 1992.

b) 4...♘g6 and now:

b1) 5 ♘f3 ♗b4+ (5...♗c5 eyeing up the dark-square weakness as quickly as possible is more logical) 6 ♘c3 ♕e7 7 ♗d3 d6 8 0-0 ♗xc3 (this opens up too many lines for White) 9 bxc3 ♘f6 10 ♗a3 c5 (10...♘xf4 11 e5 and White's bishops come into their own) 11 e5 (White forces the position open anyway and effectively demonstrates exactly what Black must strive to avoid in this variation) 11...dxe5 12 fxe5 ♘d7 13 e6 fxe6 14 ♗xg6+ hxg6 15 ♕d3 (Black's play has been a disaster) 15...0-0 16 ♕xg6 and White has an excellent position, Vogt-Hoi, Tåstrup 1990.

b2) 5 ♗e3 ♘h6 (a straightforward alternative to this interesting move is 5...♗b4+ 6 c3 ♗a5 intending ...♗b6) 6 ♕d2 f5 (this is a double-edged plan; Black is hoping to obtain superiority in the centre, but he must be very careful as his development lags) 7 ♗d3 fxe4 8 ♗xe4 ♕f6 9 ♘c3 c6 10 ♗d4 ♕f7 11 0-0-0 ♗e7 12 ♘f3 0-0 13 ♗xg6 (this is adventurous play from White but if he reconciles himself to 13 g3, then Black obtains a perfectly good position with 13...d5) 13...♕xg6 14 g4 ♕f7 15 ♖de1 ♗b4 with unclear play as in Roschina-Vlasov, Moscow 1994.

| 4 | ... | ♘xf3+ |
|---|-----|-------|
| 5 | ♕xf3 | ♕f6 |

**6    ♕g3**

6 ♕xf6 is much too simple to create any real problems for Black, e.g. 6...♘xf6 7 ♗d3 (7 ♘c3 ♗b4 8 ♗d2 0-0 9 f3 d6 10 ♘b5 ♗xd2+ 11 ♔xd2 ♘e8 12 a4 ♗e6 13 a5 a6 14 ♘d4 c5 15 ♘e2 d5 16 exd5 ♗xd5 and Black has nothing to complain about, Vujadinovic-Mestrovic, Yugoslav Ch 1991) 7...d5 8 ♘d2 ♗e6 9 exd5 ♘xd5 10 a3 0-0-0 11 ♘e4 h6 12 ♗d2 f5 13 ♘c3 g6 14 0-0-0 ♗g7 15 ♗c4 ♘f4 16 ♗xe6+ ♘xe6 17 ♘e2 again with complete equality, Westerinen-Yermolinsky, Moscow OL 1994.

**6    ...    ♕g6**

An alternative is 6...♗b4+ 7 c3 ♗d6 8 f4 ♕g6 9 ♗d3 ♕xg3+ 10 hxg3 ♗c5 11 ♘d2 d6 12 ♘c4 a6 13 a4 ♘f6 14 ♗e3 ♗xe3 15 ♘xe3 ♗d7 16 ♘d5 ♘xd5 17 exd5 a5 18 ♔f2 ♔e7 19 ♖ae1+ ½-½ Hübner-Hort, Oslo 1984.

**7    ♕xc7**

This is obviously risky, but it is the only way White can try to play for the advantage.

**7    ...    ♗d6!**

Playing the position as a gambit is Black's best approach. 7...♕xe4+ 8 ♗e3 gives White the chance to develop an initiative.

**8   ♕c4        ♘f6**
**9   ♘c3**

9 f3? runs into the strange tactic 9...♗xh2!.

**9   ...        ♗e5**

This move is positionally well motivated but Black may do better to launch an attack as quickly as possible, e.g. 9...0-0 10 f4 (simple development from White allows Black to achieve what he wants, e.g. 10 ♗e3 ♖e8 11 ♖d1 ♗e5 and Black will regain his pawn as the trick 12 f3 ♗xh2 is always in the position) 10...b5 (it is imperative for Black to play as actively as possible) 11 ♘xb5 ♘xe4 12 ♗d3 ♖e8 and Black's lead in development easily compensates his pawn deficit.

**10   ♗d2?!**

10 ♗e3 is a better test of Black's idea. White should not be concerned about Black capturing on c3 and then e4 as White would then have the two bishops in an open position and all the chances. Play can continue 10...0-0 11 0-0-0 d6 when Black has some counterplay but White should be better.

**10   ...        0-0**
**11   0-0-0**

**11   ...        d5!?**

Jadoul plays this game with tremendous energy. A more restrained approach with 11...d6 was possible but then White, as in the previous note, should stand slightly better. Jadoul is prepared to gambit most of his queenside in the interest of opening lines against the white queenside.

**12   exd5**

After 12 ♘xd5 Jadoul gives a demonstration of the Black's chances with the variations 12...♘xd5 13 exd5 (13 ♕xd5 ♕f6 14 ♕b3 ♗e6 15 ♕a3 ♕xf2) 13...♗f5 14 ♗d3 ♖fc8 15 ♗xf5 ♕xf5 16 ♕b3 b5!

planning ...♖c4, ...♖ac8 and
...a5 and in both cases Black has
promising play.

| 12 | ... | b5 |

**13    ♘xb5?**

White is determined to take
everything thrown at him, but
this is a little too greedy. With
the restrained 13 ♕b3! b4 14
♘a4 ♗f5 15 ♗d3 ♗xd3 16
♕xd3 ♕xd3 17 cxd3 ♘xd5
White would have good endgame chances. A plan here is 18
♔c2!? intending ♔b3.

Instead 13 ♕xb5 is also unnecessarily gluttonous. A possible variation is then 13...♖b8 14
♕a5 (14 ♕a4 ♗d7 15 ♕a5 ♗f5
16 ♕a4 is a way to draw immediately) 14...♗f5 15 ♕a4
♘xd5! 16 ♘xd5 ♗xb2+ 17
♔b1 ♗a3+ 18 ♔a1 with a draw
as 18 ♗b4? ♗xb4 19 ♘xb4
♗xc2+! 20 ♕xc2 ♖xb4+ 21
♔c1 ♕g5+ 22 ♖d2 ♕e5 23 ♖d1
♖b7 is good for Black.

| 13 | ... | ♗f5 |
| 14 | ♗c3 | |

14 ♗d3? ♖fc8 15 ♗xf5 ♕xf5

16 ♕b3 ♖ab8 leaves White
without a decent move.

| 14 | ... | ♖fc8 |
| 15 | ♕a4 | a6! |
| 16 | ♘d4 | |

**16    ...    ♖xc3!**

This wonderful sacrifice from
Jadoul is a fitting conclusion to
his imaginative play. Although
Black is vastly behind on material, the white position is a
wreck and he is unable to co-
ordinate his forces in time to
beat off the black attack.

**17    bxc3**

After 17 ♘xf5 ♕xf5 18 bxc3
♘e4! despite being the exchange and three pawns down,
Black has a crushing attack. The
co-ordination of Black's forces
creates a powerful impression.

| 17 | ... | ♖b8! |
| 18 | ♘b3 | |

18 ♘xf5 ♕xf5 leaves White
floundering hopelessly against a
coming check on the c1-h6 diagonal, e.g. 19 ♗d3 ♕f4+! 20
♕xf4 ♗xf4+ 21 ♖d2 ♘xd5 and
Black wins.

| 18 | ... | ♘e4! |

White has managed to close down the action of the black rook on the b-file but his position remains a mess. Meanwhile, Black is guaranteed to regain much of his sacrificed material thanks to the threats against c3 and f2.

| 19 | ♕xa6 |

It is very difficult to find a way for White to defend, e.g. 19 g3 (planning to meet checks on the c1-h6 diagonal with f4) 19...♘xf2! 20 ♖e1 (if 20 ♗xa6 ♗xc2 21 ♖de1 ♗xb3 22 axb3 ♕g5+ 23 ♔b1 ♘xh1 24 ♖xh1 ♗xc3, the white position is a disaster or 20 ♗d3 ♗xd3 21 cxd3 ♘xh1 22 ♖xh1 ♕xd3 and again Black regains virtually all of his material and the white king is left defenceless) 20...♘e4! (it is surprising that Black should expend two moves simply capturing the white f-pawn, but now the weakness on the c1-h6 diagonal is again opened up and meanwhile

White has not improved his position) 21 ♕xa6 (there is nothing better) 21...♕g5+ 22 ♔b1 ♕d2 23 ♗d3 ♘xc3+ and White will soon be mated.

| 19 | ... | ♕g5+ |
| 20 | ♔b2 | ♘xc3 |
| 21 | ♖e1 | ♕d2 |

The invasion of White's queenside is complete. There is no defence to the massed black forces.

| 22 | ♗d3 | ♘e2+ |
| 23 | ♔b1 | ♕c3 |
| | 0-1 | |

Game 21
**Howell-Miles**
*Isle of Man 1995*

| 1 | e4 | ♘c6 |
| 2 | d4 | e5 |
| 3 | dxe5 | ♘xe5 |
| 4 | ♘c3 | |

With this move White avoids the inconvenience of the bishop thrust (4...♗b4 is well met by 5 ♕d4) and keeps his options open as to how to deal with

Black's central knight.

**4 ... ♗c5**

This is the most logical move. Black develops a piece, does not yet commit the king's knight and keeps the h4-d8 diagonal open to develop his queen.

**5 ♗f4**

A more adventurous, but also more risky try is 5 f4, e.g. 5...♘c6 6 ♗c4 (incidentally threatening ♗xf7+) 6...d6 7 ♘f3 ♗e6 8 ♗xe6 fxe6 9 ♘a4 ♗b6 10 ♘xb6 axb6 and the position was unclear in Akopian-

Miles, Moscow 1990.

**5 ... d6**

5...♘g6 6 ♗g3 d6 7 h4 (7 ♕d2 ♘f6 8 0-0-0 0-0 9 ♗c4 is an alternative scheme of development) 7...h5 8 ♕d2 ♘f6 9 0-0-0 ♗d7 (9...♕e7 10 ♘d5 ♘xd5 11 exd5 0-0 left Black permanently hampered by his weak kingside in Dolmatov-Gulko, Hastings 1989: 12 ♗e2 ♗g4 13 ♗xg4 hxg4 14 h5 ♘e5 15 ♗h4 ♕d7 16 h6 ♕f5 17 hxg7 ♔xg7 18 ♘e2 ♖h8 19 ♘g3 ♕g6 20 ♕f4 f6 21 ♘e4 ♖af8 22 ♘xc5 dxc5 23 ♗g3 ♖xh1 24 ♖xh1 ♖d8 25 ♕a4 ♖xd5 26 ♕xa7 ♕g5+ 27 ♔b1 ♕d2 28 a3 ♕e2 29 ♕xb7 ♖d1+ 30 ♖xd1 ♕xd1+ 31 ♔a2 and White went on to win) 10 f3 ♕e7 11 ♔b1 0-0-0 12 ♘ge2 (White has a space advantage but the black position is very solid) 12...♘e5 13 ♘d4 ♘c6 14 ♘xc6 ♗xc6 15 ♗c4 ♗b4 (Black frees his position with exchanges) 16 ♕d3 ♗xc3 17 ♕xc3 ♘d7 18 ♗d5 ♗xd5 19 ♖xd5 ♘b6 20 ♖a5 ♔b8 21 ♗f2 f6 22 ♗xb6 axb6 23 ♖b5 ♕d7 24 ♕b3 ♖de8 25 ♖d1 ♖e5 26 a4 ♖he8 27 ♖dd5 ♖xd5 ½-½ Brinck-Claussen - Hoi, Tåstrup 1995.

Note how in these two games the black knight had very little to do on g6. Therefore Miles's continuation, maintaining this piece in the centre, seems more logical.

**6 ♕d2**

our main line move 6...♘f6.

|   |       |      |
|---|-------|------|
| 7 | 0-0-0 | ♗e6  |
| 8 | ♘a4   |      |

| 6 | ... | ♘f6 |
|---|-----|-----|

Others:

a) 6...♗e6 led to intricate play in Kazhgaleev-Vlasov, Moscow 1994: 7 h4 a6 8 h5 f6 (this is a strange move; why not 8...h6 with a perfectly reasonable position?) 9 ♘d5 c6 10 ♘e3 ♕b6 11 c3 a5 12 ♘f3 0-0-0 13 ♘d4 ♗f7 14 ♗g3 ♘h6 15 ♗e2 ♖he8 16 0-0 g6 with a complex middlegame.

b) 6...♘e7 7 0-0-0 ♗e6 8 ♘a4 (the lack of pressure against the white e-pawn - 6...♘e7 instead of 6...♘f6 - allows White to gain the bishop pair) 8...♘d7 9 ♘xc5 ♘xc5 10 f3 0-0 11 ♗e3 b6 12 ♘e2 a5 13 a3 was Ulibin-Danailov, Ibercaja 1992. White is a little better.

In his recent book, *An Opening Repertoire for the Attacking Player*, Eduard Gufeld dismisses the defence 1...♘c6 by claiming a large advantage for White in this variation. However, he only considers 6...♘e7 and does not take into account

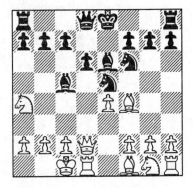

White takes advantage of a tactical feature of the position in order to gain the bishop pair.

| 8 | ... | ♗b6 |
|---|-----|-----|

Miles is happy to allow White to gain the two bishops as in return the a-file will be opened which will allow him to generate pressure against the white king. He could also have tested White's idea with 8...♘xe4, which leads to complex play, e.g. 9 ♕e1 ♘xf2 10 ♘xc5 ♘xh1 (10...♘xd1 is better and leads to an unclear position after 11 ♘xe6 fxe6 12 ♕xd1 0-0) 11 ♗b5+! (more incisive than 11 ♘xe6 fxe6 12 ♘h3) 11...c6 12 ♘xb7 ♕b6 13 ♘xd6+ ♔f8 14 ♕xe5 cxb5 15 ♗e3 and White is winning.

| 9  | f3 | 0-0  |
|----|----|------|
| 10 | a3 | ♕e7  |

The black opening has been a complete success. He is fully developed and has attacking chances on the queenside.

| | 11 | ♘xb6 | axb6 |
| | 12 | ♘e2 |

**12 ... ♘g6!**

It looks strange to retreat the knight from its fine central position, but Miles wants to play ...d5. This advance will clear the centre and allow him to feed pieces swiftly over to the queenside. White is already in big trouble.

**13 ♔b1**

If 13 ♘c3 then 13...♖a5.

| | 13 | ... | d5 |
| | 14 | exd5 | ♘xd5 |

**15 ♕c1**

This is too passive to give White chances of beating off the black attack. White could have tried for a tactical solution to his problems with 15 ♗g5 but this also looks unpromising, e.g. 15...f6 (15...♕c5 16 ♘d4 gives White chances to defend) 16 ♘d4 ♗f7 and now White has various tactical tries but they ultimately fail: 17 ♗h6!? (17 c4 fxg5 18 cxd5 ♗xd5 is very good for Black) 17...♕d7! (this is more accurate than 17...gxh6 which becomes messy after 18 ♘f5 ♕c5 19 ♘xh6+ ♔g7 20 ♘xf7 ♘e3 21 b4!) 18 c4 (forced) 18...gxh6 19 cxd5 ♕xd5 and Black stands well.

**15 ... b5**

The advance of this pawn will completely open the white king's defences. White is already completely lost.

| | 16 | ♗d2 | b4 |
| | 17 | axb4 | ♘xb4 |

**18 b3**

Other tries also succumb

quickly: 18 ♘c3 ♘a2 19 ♘xa2 ♗xa2+ 20 ♔a1 ♕e6 and White has no way to meet the threat of ...♗b1+ or 18 ♗xb4 ♗a2+ 19 ♔a1 ♕xb4 and the white king sill not survive long.

| 18 | ... | ♘xc2! |
|---|---|---|
| 19 | ♕xc2 | |

19 ♔xc2 ♖a2+ 20 ♔b1 ♖fa8 with ...♖a1+ and ...♗f5+ on the cards.

| 19 | ... | ♕a3 |
|---|---|---|

| 20 | ♕c3 |
|---|---|

After 20 ♗c3 one way to win is 20...♗xb3 21 ♕d2 ♗a2+ 22 ♔c2 ♕b3+ 23 ♔d3 ♖ad8+ 24 ♘d4 ♖fe8.

| 20 | ... | ♗f5+ |
|---|---|---|
| **0-1** | | |

A well played game by Miles and an excellent advert for the black system.

Game 22
**Campora-Miles**
*Seville 1993*

| 1 | e4 | ♘c6 |
|---|---|---|
| 2 | d4 | e5 |

| 3 | d5 |
|---|---|

| 3 | ... | ♘ce7 |
|---|---|---|

White's most usual continuation here is 4 c4, transposing into the variation 1 d4 ♘c6 2 c4 e5 3 d5 ♘ce7 4 e4, examined in chapter five. Here we consider attempts by White either to delay c4 substantially, or to get by without it altogether.

| 4 | ♗e3 |
|---|---|

4 ♘f3 ♘g6 5 h4 led to obscure play in Mortensen-Hoi, Ostrava 1992: 5...h5 6 ♘c3 (this looks better than 6 ♗g5 ♗e7 7 g3 d6 8 ♘bd2 ♗g4 9 ♗b5+ ♔f8 10 ♗e2 a6 11 a4 ♘f6 12 ♗xf6 ♗xf6 13 ♘h2 ♗xe2 14 ♕xe2 and Black had no problems, Ostojic-Kaulfuss, Hessen 1991) 6...♗b4 (this leaves the black h-pawn rather exposed and so 6...♗e7 may be better) 7 ♗g5 ♘f6 8 ♘d2 c6 9 ♗e2 ♗xc3 10 bxc3 cxd5 11 ♗xh5 ♘f4 12 ♗f3 ♘e6 13 ♗xf6 ♕xf6 14 exd5 ♘c5 15 g3 d6 with some counterplay for the pawn.

**4    ...    f5**

The positioning of the white bishop on e3 acts as a target for this advance.

**5  f3        ♘f6**
**6  ♘c3**

Or 6 ♗d3 f4 7 ♗f2 g5 8 c4 (8 h4!?) 8...♘g6 9 ♘c3 ♗b4 (Black is playing the position like a King's Indian but, having not yet committed his bishop to g7, he finds a more useful role for this piece) 10 ♕b3 ♕e7 11 0-0-0 ♗c5 12 ♗xc5 ♕xc5 13 ♔b1 d6 (having exchanged his inferior dark-squared bishop, Black has a very comfortable game) 14 ♘ge2 ♕b6 15 ♕c2 ♗d7 16 ♔a1 ♔e7 (there is no need for Black to castle and he wants to keep the g-file free for his rooks) 17 ♘c1 g4 18 ♕e2 ♖hg8 19 ♘b3 gxf3 20 gxf3.

White is hoping for counterplay based on c5, but Black keeps everything under control with a clever pawn sacrifice: 20...♕e3! 21 ♕xe3 fxe3 22 ♖de1 (now Black will lose his advanced e-pawn but his invasion along the g-file means that the white h-pawn is, in the long term, indefensible) 22...♘f4 23 ♖xe3 ♖g5 24 a3 (White is very tangled up and the attempt to expel the black knight with 24 ♘e2 leaves the white rook entombed after the response 24...♘g2) 24...♖ag8 25 c5 ♖g1+ 26 ♖xg1 ♖xg1+ 27 ♔a2 ♖h1 28 ♗b5 ♖xh2 29 ♘a5 ♗c8 30 cxd6+ cxd6 and the black h-pawn proved to be the decisive factor, Paramos-Izeta, Spanish Ch. 1993.

**6    ...        d6**
**7  ♕d2      g6**
**8  0-0-0    ♗g7**

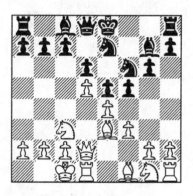

**9  h3**

White is hoping to gain space on the kingside by advancing g4, but Black's reply cuts across this plan.

**9    ...        f4!**
**10  ♗f2      0-0**
**11  ♔b1      a6**
**12  ♘ge2    ♗d7**
**13  ♘c1**

| 17 | dxc6 | ♘xc6 |
|----|------|------|
| 18 | ♘xc6 | ♗xc6 |
| 19 | ♗h4 | ♖d7 |
| 20 | ♗xf6 | ♗xf6 |
| 21 | ♘d5 | |

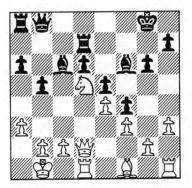

| 13 | ... | b5 |
|----|-----|-----|

This is perfectly playable but it leaves Black's queenside a little exposed. An alternative plan was 13...♘c8, defending the d-pawn and planning to break with ...c5. White now conceives of a plan to manoeuvre his pieces around to the queenside in the hope of exploiting the slight Black weaknesses there.

| 14 | a3 | ♕b8 |
|----|-----|-----|
| 15 | ♘b3 | ♖d8 |

Black employs an alternative method of defending his d-pawn in preparation for ...c5.

| 16 | ♘a5 | c5 |
|----|------|-----|

Black has been angling for this break but White's 19th move leaves him in control of the important d5-square. Therefore Black might have done better to wait with 16...h6, preventing the plan White now carries out. It is difficult to see how White can then improve his position before Black plays ...c5 on his next move.

| 21 | ... | ♗h4 |
|----|-----|-----|

The bishop appears out of play here but if Black ever has the chance to play ...♗f2, it will have a wonderful diagonal to work on.

| 22 | ♘b4 | ♗b7 |
|----|------|------|
| 23 | c4 | ♔g7 |
| 24 | ♗d3 | |

Here White goes astray and the black position comes to life. White should have preferred 24 cxb5 axb5 25 ♗d3 (but not 25 ♗xb5 ♗xe4+ 26 fxe4 ♕xb5 when the unhappy position of the white king gives Black all the chances) 25...♕a7 26 ♖hf1 preventing ...♗f2 and keeping the position balanced.

| 24 | ... | a5! |
|----|-----|-----|

This is very sharp play from Miles. With the aid of a pawn sacrifice, Black's whole position now comes to life.

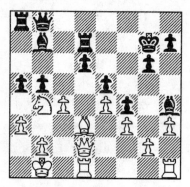

| 25 | ♘a2 | b4! |
| 26 | axb4 | axb4 |
| 27 | ♕xb4 | |

Instead 27 ♘xb4 ♕a7 threatens, amongst others, ...♗f2 and if 28 ♖hf1 then 28...♗d8! and with the bishop coming round to b6 or a5, White has big problems.

| 27 | ... | ♗f2! |
| 28 | ♘c3 | ♗d4 |

This fabulous outpost for the bishop is worth much more than the sacrificed pawn.

| 29 | ♔c2 | ♕c8 |
| 30 | ♘b5 | ♗c5 |

| 31 | ♕b3 | ♗a6 |

Black now always has the option of ...♗xb5 when the resulting opposite-coloured bishops position greatly favour the attacking player.

| 32 | ♖a1 | ♗e3 |
| 33 | ♖hd1 | ♖b7 |
| 34 | ♘xd6? | |

White, under heavy pressure, blunders and loses immediately. His best try was 34 ♔b1 when Black has the pleasant choice between 34...♗xb5 at once, or keeping the tension with 34...♖b6, planning to increase the pressure with ...♕c5 or ...♕b7.

| 34 | ... | ♖xb3 |

White had no doubt calculated 34...♖xb3 35 ♘xc8 ♖xd3 36 ♖xd3 when Black is unable to recapture the knight on c8. Unfortunately he had overlooked 34...♖xb3 35 ♘xc8 ♖ab8! when the knight on c8 is lost as 36 ♖xa6 gets mated after 36...♖xb2+ 37 ♔c3 ♖8b3.

**0-1**

**Transposition to the Scotch**

Game 23
**Hort-Xie Jun**
*Prague (Women v Veterans)*
*1995*

| 1 | e4 | ♘c6 |
|---|-----|------|
| 2 | d4 | e5 |
| 3 | ♘f3 | |

With this move White turns the game into the Scotch Opening. Although readers may consider the Scotch Opening to be outside the parameters of this book, transposition into this opening is an option for White if Black plays the move we consider most promising here, i.e. 2...e5. Therefore in this game and the next we recommend defences for Black against the two main variations of the Scotch.

| 3 | ... | exd4 |
|---|--------|------|
| 4 | ♘xd4 | ♘f6 |
| 5 | ♘xc6 | |

In the next game we consider White's alternative of 5 ♘c3.

| 5 | ... | bxc6 |
|---|------|------|
| 6 | e5 | ♕e7 |
| 7 | ♕e2 | ♘d5 |
| 8 | c4 | ♗a6 |

**9 b3**

White has various other possibilities here:

a) 9 ♕e4 suggests that White is content with a draw as Black can reply 9...♘f6 10 ♕e2 ♘d5 repeating the position. However, Black is not obliged to acquiesce in a draw, e.g. 11 ♕e4 ♘b6 12 ♘d2 0-0-0 13 b3 f6 (the black queenside pieces are temporarily locked out of the game but White is under-developed and his centre is vulnerable) 14 f4 fxe5 15 fxe5 d5 16 cxd5 ♗xf1 17 ♖xf1 cxd5 18 ♕g4+ ♚b7 19 ♗b2 h5 20 ♕e2 ♕e6 (Black has very good chances) 21 0-0-0 ♗e7 22 ♘f3 c5 (by preventing the white knight from coming to d4, Black maintains the central blockade) 23 h4 ♕g4 24 ♕c2 ♖h6! (an excellent way to complete the mobilisation of his forces) 25 ♔b1 ♖c6 26 ♗c1 d4 27 ♕d3 a5 28 ♘g5 ♘d5 29 ♗d2 c4 (it looks as though this attacking plan will expose both kings but the key features are Black's central control and the excellent co-ordination of his forces which allow him to benefit from the opening of the position) 30 bxc4 ♘e3 31 ♗xa5 ♖b8 32 ♔a1 ♔a8 33 g3 ♖a6 34 ♗c7

34...♖a3! 35 ♕g6 ♖xa2+ 0-1 Gavrilakis-Wahls, Haifa 1989.

b) 9 ♘d2 ♘b4 (with this move Black plans to regroup with ...c5 and ...♘c6 but an alternative is 9...g6) 10 ♕e4 ♘b6 11 ♗d3 ♗g7 12 0-0 0-0 13 f4 d6 (Black must counter quickly in the centre and he is not afraid of 14 ♕xc6 as he gains the initiative after 14...dxe5 14 ♘f3 dxe5 and Black has a promising position as 15 f5 runs into the tactic 15 f5 ♗xc4 16 ♗xc4 ♕c5+) 10 ♘f3 c5 11 a3 ♘c6 12 ♗d2 d5 13 exd6 ♕xe2+ 14 ♗xe2 ♗xd6 15 b4 ♗b7 16 ♖b1

0-0-0 17 0-0 ♖he8 18 ♖fe1 f6 and Black has a solid position, J. Polgar-Piket Aruba 1995.

**9 ... ♕h4**

This is a tricky tactical move which threatens to invade the white position with a combination of ...♕d4 and ...♗b4+. White's passive reply is more or less forced.

**10 a3 ♗c5**
**11 ♗b2**

White has two other tries:

a) If White tries to expel the black queen from her post with 11 g3

he runs into the surprising tactic 11...♗xf2+! which nets one of the white rooks and leads to complex play, e.g. 12 ♕xf2 (or 12 ♔xf2 ♕d4+ 13 ♔g2 ♕xa1 and it is difficult for White to justify his material deficit, e.g. 14 ♕c2 ♕xe5 15 ♗d3 ♘e3+ 16 ♗xe3 ♕xe3 17 ♕c3 0-0-0 18 ♖e1 ♕h6 19 ♕a5 c5 20 ♕xc5 ♗b7+ 21 ♗e4 ♗xe4+ 22 ♖xe4 ♕c6 23 ♕xc6 dxc6 24 ♖e3 ♖he8 25 ♖f3 ♖e2+ 26 ♔h3 ♖b2 0-1 Tomczak-Lukacs, Bundesliga 1995) 12...♕e4+ 13 ♔d2 ♕xh1 14 ♗g2 ♕xh2 15 cxd5 cxd5 (White has regained some material but his exposed king gives Black good play) 16 ♔c2 (16 ♘c3 c6 17 ♗b2 ♕h6+ 18 ♕f4 is unclear) 16...c6 17 ♗e3 ♕h5 18 ♘c3 0-0 19 ♗d4 ♖fe8 20 ♔b2 ♗d3 21 ♖h1 ♕g5 22 ♗h3 ♖ad8 23 ♖d1 ♗a6 24 ♖d2 d6 (Black breaks White's central blockade and opens lines for the rooks) 25 exd6 ♖xd6 26 ♕f4 ♕xf4 27 gxf4 ♖h6 28 ♗f5 ♗f1 29 ♖f2 ♗h3 30 ♗xh3 ♖xh3 31 ♗xa7 h5 32 f5 ♖h1 33 ♗d4 ♔h7 34 ♖g2 g6 and Black went on to win, M. Maric-Voiska, Subotica IZ 1991.

b) 11 ♕f3 ♘e7 and White must be careful as his position is somewhat underdeveloped. For example, after the over-ambitious 12 b4? Black hits back with 12...♕d4 13 ♖a2 ♗xc4! 14 ♖d2 ♕xe5+ 15 ♔d1 ♗d5 16 ♖xd5 ♘xd5 17 bxc5 0-0 18 ♗d3 f5! (Black has an excellent position as the white king is so exposed) 19 ♗c4 ♔h8 20 ♗xd5 cxd5 21 ♕d3 ♖ab8 22 ♖e1 ♕xh2 23 ♘c3 ♕xg2 24 ♕xd5 ♕xf2 25 ♖e2 ♕f1+ 26 ♔c2 f4 27 ♖e7 f3? (a mistake which allows White to draw; the simple 27...♕g1 would have prevented White's next and left Black with good winning chances) 28 ♖xg7 ♕f2+ 29 ♔d3 ♕f1+ ½-½ Yakovich-Emelin, St Petersburg 1995.

**11 ... ♘f4**

**12 ♕f3**

White must be careful here. For example the natural 12 ♕d2? loses immediately to the tactical trick 12...♘h3! 13 gxh3 ♕e4+.

**12 ... ♘e6**
**13 g3**

White is anxious to expel the black queen but also possible is 13 ♗d3 ♗d4 14 ♖a2 with an unclear position.

**13 ... ♘g5**

This is a complex position and there are two other moves which should also be considered by Black. We give both of them as they demonstrate typical methods by which Black can exploit his active pieces in this variation:

a) 13...♕h6 14 ♕d1 (14 ♘d2 0-0 15 ♘e4 ♖ab8 16 ♘xc5 ♘xc5 17 b4 ♘a4 18 ♗c1 ♕e6 19 ♕e4 - Black has developed all his pieces whereas White only has the queen in play so it is not surprising that Black opens the position and quickly gains a decisive advantage - 19...c5 20 ♗d3 f5 21 exf6 ♕xe4+ 22 ♗xe4 ♖be8 23 f3 ♗xc4 24 bxc5 ♘xc5 25 ♗e3 ♘xe4 26 fxe4 ♖xe4 and Black soon won, Ocytko-Aleksandrov, Wisla 1992) 14...f6 (White's dark-square weaknesses become apparent after this pawn break) 15 exf6 0-0 16 ♗e2 ♖xf6 17 0-0 (17 ♗xf6 ♕xf6 hits a1 and f2 and wins immediately, but the move played does not help) 17...♖xf2 18 ♖xf2 ♖f8 19 b4 ♖xf2 0-1 Edvardsson-Carlhammar, Gausdal 1992.

b) 13...♕e7 also looks promising, e.g. 14 ♘d2 0-0-0 15 b4 (15 ♗g2 ♘d4 16 ♕e4 d5! 17 exd6 ♕xd6 18 0-0 ♖he8 and Black wins due to the threat of ...♘e2+) 15...♗d4 16 ♗xd4? (a blunder but the position was difficult for White anyway) 16...♘xd4 17 ♕e4 ♘c2+! and the white rook on a1 goes after

18 ♕xc2 ♕xe5+, Gomez-Valdes, Cuba 1991.

**14  ♕e2**

14 ♕xf7+ ♔xf7 15 gxh4 ♘f3+ 16 ♔d1 ♖ae8 17 ♘d2 ♗d4 18 ♗xd4 ♘xd4 19 f4 ♖hf8 and the white pawns are exposed in the endgame.

**14  ...  ♕e4**
**15  ♕xe4  ♘xe4**

**16  f4?**

With so many pieces undeveloped, this move is a luxury that White cannot afford. He had to play more actively with 16 f3 ♘f2 17 b4 ♗e3 when the

line given by Blatny is 18 c5!
♘d3+ (not 18...♗xf1 19 ♖xf1
♘d3+ when the white king
charges up the board to good
effect, e.g. 20 ♔e2 ♘xb2 21
♔xe3 d5 22 exd6 cxd6 23 cxd6
♘c4+ 24 ♔d4 ♘xd6 25 ♔c5)
19 ♗xd3 ♗xd3 20 ♘c3 0-0-0
with an unclear position.

**16 ... ♖b8!**

Now the black pieces become
too active and White cannot
cope with all the threats. Not so
good is 16...♘f2 17 b4 ♗e3 18
♔e2 ♗b6 as White now has the
clever move 19 ♔e1! threatening c5 and Black has nothing
better than 19...♗e3 repeating
moves.

**17 b4 ♗f2+**
**18 ♔d1**

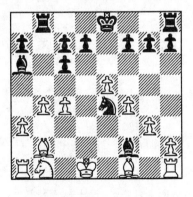

**18 ... ♗xg3!**
**19 ♖g1**

This is a desperate attempt to
stir up complications, but after
19 hxg3 ♘f2+ 20 ♔e2 ♘xh1 21
♔f3 c5! 22 b5 ♗b7+ Black res-
cues the knight with a winning
position.

**19 ... ♗xf4**
**20 ♖xg7 ♔e7**
**21 ♗g2?**

This loses the exchange but
after 21 ♖g2 ♖hg8 Black is a
pawn up with a good position
and should win easily.

**21 ... ♗h6**
**22 ♗xe4 ♗xg7**
**23 ♘d2**

White is hoping to create
chances of saving the game
based on the temporary lack of
co-ordination of the black
forces but Xie Jun easily pre-
vents White becoming too active.

**23 ... f6**

With her extra exchange
Black concentrates on opening
up files as quickly as possible.
The resulting slight exposure of
her king is of minimal importance.

**24 exf6+ ♗xf6**
**25 ♗xf6+ ♔xf6**
**26 ♔c2 ♖be8**
**27 ♖f1+ ♔e7**

Black's only remaining task
now is to activate her dormant
queen's bishop.

**28 ♖f5 ♔d8**
**29 ♗d3 ♗c8**
**30 ♖a5 a6**
**31 ♖h5**

31 c5 is perhaps an improve-
ment but it does not help after
31...d5 32 cxd6 cxd6 33 ♗xa6
♗xa6 34 ♖xa6 ♔d7 and Black
wins.

**31 ... d6**
**32 ♘e4 ♖e5**

| 33 | ♖xe5 | dxe5 |
|----|------|------|
| 34 | ♘g5 | ♔e7 |

**35 ♗xh7?**

From the perspective of avoiding tactical traps, this has not been one of Hort's better games. However 35 ♘xh7 ♗e6 36 c5 ♗g8 37 ♘g5 ♖xh2+ was also hopeless.

| 35 | ... | ♖xh7 |

**0-1**

After 36 ♘xh7 ♗f5+ picks up the knight.

### Game 24
### Golubev-Malaniuk
*Alushta 1994*

| 1 | e4 | ♘c6 |
|----|------|------|
| 2 | d4 | e5 |
| 3 | ♘f3 | exd4 |
| 4 | ♘xd4 | |

There are a couple of gambit tries here for White which need to be considered:

a) The Göring Gambit is brought into play with 4 c3. A safe line for Black here is 4...d5 5 exd5 ♕xd5 6 cxd4 ♗g4 7 ♗e2 ♗b4+ 8 ♘c3 ♗xf3 9 ♗xf3 ♕c4 10 ♗xc6+ (10 ♕b3 ♕xb3 11 axb3 ♘ge7 leaves White with a feeble pawn structure) 10...bxc6 11 ♕e2+ ♕xe2 12 ♔xe2 0-0-0 and many games have shown that Black has a very pleasant position.

b) 4 ♗c4 is an attempt to transpose to variations such as the Giuoco Piano or Two Knights Defence. One way for Black to avoid these is 4...♗c5 5 c3 d3, e.g. 6 b4 (White can play more safely by not expanding on the queenside, but then Black has a comfortable game) 6...♗b6 7 ♕b3 ♕e7 8 0-0 d6 9 a4 a6 10 a5 ♗a7 11 b5 axb5 12 ♗xb5. *ECO* mysteriously assesses this position as clearly better for White, but, after the simple 12...♘f6, this seems wrong, e.g. 13 e5 dxe5 14 ♗a3 ♕e6 15 ♗c4 ♕d7 16 ♖e1 e4, Emmerich-Kaulfuss, Hessen 1988 or 13 a6 0-0 14 ♗xd3 ♗b6 15 ♘bd2 bxa6 16 ♘c4 ♗c5, Roeberg-Kaulfuss, Bundesliga 1994 and in both cases Black stands much better.

| 4 | ... | ♘f6 |
|----|------|------|
| 5 | ♘c3 | ♗b4 |
| 6 | ♘xc6 | bxc6 |
| 7 | ♗d3 | d5 |
| 8 | exd5 | cxd5 |
| 9 | 0-0 | 0-0 |
| 10 | ♗g5 | c6 |
| 11 | ♘a4 | |

This variation has recently gained popularity. White concedes the centre, but gains active piece play in return. This can manifest itself in the form of an attack with pieces on the kingside or an attempt to gain play in the centre with c4 (or perhaps c3 and ♗e3, playing for a blockade).

In the following analysis we see White attempting to play along the former lines.

a) 11 ♘e2 (White intends to route this knight around to the kingside via d4 and f5) 11...h6 12 ♗h4 ♗d6 (another way for Black to play is to break the pin with 12...♗e7) 13 ♘d4 ♗d7 14 c3 ♖e8 15 ♕c2 ♘h5 16 ♗xe7 ♕xe7 (Black has comfortably equalised and now takes the initiative on the kingside) 17 ♗e2 ♘f4 18 ♗f3 ♕g5 19 g3 c5 20 ♘e2 ♗f5 21 ♕d1 ♘h3+ 22 ♔h1 ♖ad8 23 ♘g1 d4 24 cxd4 cxd4 25 ♖c1 ♘xg1 26 ♔xg1 ♗h3 27 ♖e1 d3 28 ♕a4 ♕xc1 0-1 was Weinzettl-Dobrovolsky, Oberwart 1991) 13 ♘d4 c5 14 ♘f5

this bishop with 14...♗e5 15 c3 when the position is equal, Ljubojevic-P. Nikolic, Wijk aan Zee 1988) 15 ♗xf5 ♖b8 (it is a typical theme of this variation that the white queenside can become exposed) 16 b3 ♗e5 17 ♖b1 ♕d6 18 ♗g3 ♗xg3 19 hxg3 ♖fe8 (Black has co-ordinated his forces and now stands better thanks to his central control) 20 ♖e1 ♖xe1+ 21 ♕xe1 ♖e8 22 ♕d2 ♕e5 23 ♕f4 ♕c3 24 ♖f1 g6 25 ♗d3 ♔g7 26 f3 a5 and Black has a useful initiative, Lutz-Yusupov, Munich 1992.

b) 11 ♕f3 ♗e7

(it is a perfectly reasonable idea for Black to allow the doubling of the f-pawns - with ♗xf6 - but here he chooses to prevent this possibility while also breaking the pin on his knight) 12 ♖ae1 ♖e8 13 ♘e2 (13 h3 ♗e6 14 ♘e2 ♘d7 15 ♗xe7 ♕xe7 16 ♘d4 ♕b4 17 ♘xe6 ♖xe6 18 ♖xe6 fxe6 19 ♕e3 ♘f8 20 ♕e5 ♕b8 21 ♖e1

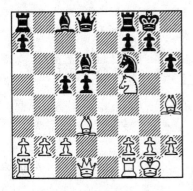

14...♗xf5 (Black can save

♕xe5 22 ♖xe5 ♖b8 23 b3 ♔f7
and the black centre pawns give
him the edge in the endgame,
Rotman-Smyslov, Rishon le
Zion 1993) 13...h6 14 ♗f4 ♗d6
15 ♘d4 ♗g4 16 ♕g3 ♗xf4 17
♕xf4 ♕b6 18 c4 ♗d7 19 cxd5
cxd5 20 ♖xe8+ ♖xe8 21 ♕d2
♘e4 22 ♗xe4 dxe4 23 b3 ♖d8

was the continuation of the
5th game from the Deep Blue-
Kasparov match in Philadelphia
1996. The position is fine for
Black and Kasparov offered a
draw. However, the Deep Blue
team, perhaps unwisely, de-
clined, as the position is an
open one and thus should favour the computer's enormous
calculating power: 24 ♕c3 f5
25 ♖d1? (this move will cause
White some headaches on the d-
file) 25...♗e6 26 ♕e3 (Deep
Blue still doesn't sense the danger that the pin on the d-file
poses) 26...♗f7 27 ♕c3 f4 28
♖d2 ♕f6 29 g3 ♖d5 30 a3 ♔h7
31 ♔g2 ♕e5 32 f3 e3 33 ♖d3
e2 34 gxf4 e1♕ 35 fxe5 ♕xc3

36 ♖xc3 ♖xd4 37 b4 ♗c4 38
♔f2 g5 39 ♖e3 ♖d2+ 40 ♔e1
♖d3 41 ♔f2 ♔g6 42 ♖xd3
♗xd3 43 ♔e3 ♗c2 44 ♔d4 ♔f5
45 ♔d5 h5 0-1 Deep Blue-
Kasparov, Philadelphia 1996.

| 11 | ... | h6 |
| 12 | ♗h4 | ♖e8 |

**13  c4**

This is the most thematic
continuation for White, who
hopes to mount an initiative
against the black centre. Instead
13 c3 ♗d6 is somewhat insipid,
e.g. 14 b3 ♗f4 15 ♕c2? (this
blunder loses a pawn, but Black
had nothing to complain about
anyway) 15...♗xh2+ (before
White obligingly moved his
queen to c2, this combination
would have failed as after white
captured the bishop with his
king and White replied ...♘g4+,
White would have had the
counter-stroke ♕xg4) 16 ♔h1
♗f4 17 g3 ♗d6 18 f4 c5 and
Black won easily, Lau-Piket,
Leeuwarden 1993.

| 13 | ... | ♗d6 |

Or 13...♖b8 14 ♖c1 ♗e6 15 cxd5 ♗xd5 16 b3 ♗d6 (although, theoretically, Black has slightly the worse pawn structure, the activity of his pieces and their central outposts constitute more than enough compensation) 17 ♘c3 ♖b4 18 ♗g3 (here 18 ♘xd5 runs into the tactic 18...♗xh2+!) 18...♗xg3 19 hxg3 ♗xg2! 20 ♔xg2 ♖d4 21 ♕f3 ♖xd3 22 ♕xc6 (White has maintained material equality but his kingside has been compromised) 22...♖e6 23 ♕b7 ♖e7 24 ♕b4 ♘d5 25 ♘xd5 ♕xd5+ 26 ♔g1 ♖e2 (Black's plan of centralisation is complete) 27 ♕b8+ ♔h7 28 ♕f4 ♖xa2 29 ♖ce1 ♖f3 30 ♖e5 ♕xb3 31 ♕g4 ♖axf2 0-1 was the game Schmaltz-Dubiel, Altensteig 1994. After 32 ♖xf2 ♕d1+ 33 ♔g2 ♖xf2+ the white queen is lost.

**14 cxd5**

Black also gained great activity after 14 ♖c1 ♗f4 in Zarnicki-I. Sokolov, Oviedo 1993, viz. 15 ♖c2 ♗g4 16 f3 ♗e6 17 cxd5 ♗xd5 18 ♗c4 ♕d6 19 ♗xf6 ♗xh2+ 20 ♔h1 ♕xf6 21 ♗xd5 ♗g3 22 ♖c4 cxd5 23 ♖g4 ♕e5 24 ♔g1 ♗h2+ 25 ♔h1 ♕h5 0-1.

Both this game and the previous example demonstrate the excellent positioning of the black queen's bishop on d5. Therefore White takes on d5 immediately to oblige Black to recapture with a piece. However this does not prevent Black from taking the initiative.

**14 ... cxd5**

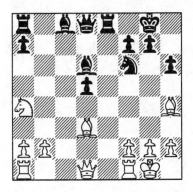

**15 ♘c3**

White has to be careful to complete his development without getting tangled up, e.g. 15 ♖c1 ♗f4 16 ♖c6 g5 17 ♗g3 ♗d7 and Black has the initiative.

**15 ... ♗e5**
**16 ♖e1**

Black's last move set a trap which White fell for in Shvidler-Malaniuk, St. Petersburg 1993, viz. 16 ♘xd5?? ♕xd5 17 ♗xf6 (White's play is based on 17...♗xf6 18 ♗h7+, but ...) 17...♗b7!. Now the queen is defended and White has no time to save his bishop due to the mate threat on g2.

**16 ... ♗b7**

Black has excellent play for his pieces.

**17 ♕d2 ♕b6**

Also possible is 17...♕d6 18 ♗g3 ♗xg3 19 hxg3 d4 20 ♘b5 ♕d5, threatening mate, with a good game.

| 18 | ♗g3 | ♗xg3 |
| 19 | hxg3 | ♘e4 |
| 20 | ♗xe4 | dxe4 |
| 21 | ♖ad1 | ♖ad8 |

Here we have the same structure as occurred in the game between Kasparov and

Deep Blue which we looked at in the note to White's 11th. Again Black stands very comfortably thanks to his extra central pawn and strong minor piece.

| 22 | ♕c1 | ♖xd1 |
| 23 | ♘xd1 | ♕a5 |
| 24 | ♘c3 | ♕b4 |
| 25 | ♕d2 | ♖e6 |
| 26 | a3 | ♕b6 |

More incisive here was 26...♕b3, maintaining pressure against White's queenside. Now White succeeds in simplifying the position to force a draw.

| 27 | b4 | ♕a6 |
| 28 | ♕d8+ | ♔h7 |
| 29 | ♕d7 | ♕xa3 |
| 30 | ♕xb7 | ♕xc3 |
|    | ½-½ |      |

# 3   1 e4 ♘c6 2 ♘f3 d6

| 1 | e4 | ♘c6 |
|---|-----|-----|
| 2 | ♘f3 | d6 |

In this variation, Black offers an immediate transposition into standard open-game territory, with 2...e5, but Black declines with our recommended continuation of 2...d6.

With this move, Black prepares to develop his queen's bishop at g4 and his knight at f6 leaving him with a very flexible position. Depending upon how White lines up his forces, he can counter in the centre with ...e6 and ...d5, the direct ...e5 or perhaps capture the f3-knight and then play ...g6, heading for a type of Pirc Defence position.

The most natural continuation (from the above diagram) is now:

| 3 | d4 | ♘f6 |
|---|-----|-----|
| 4 | ♘c3 | ♗g4 |

From this position White has three main strategies: to weaken Black's pawn structure with ♗b5 and ♗xc6, to break the pin on his f3-knight with 5 ♗e2 or finally, to develop with 5 ♗e3 and hope to find a more active role for the king's bishop. All of these strategies, and the correct ways for Black to counter them, are examined in the following games.

Game 25
**Tseshkovsky-Miles**
*Palma de Mallorca 1989*

| 1 | e4 | ♘c6 |
|---|-----|-----|

| 2 | ♘f3 | d6 |
| 3 | d4 | ♘f6 |
| 4 | ♘c3 | ♗g4 |
| 5 | ♗e3 | e6 |

**6  h3**

Putting the question immediately to Black's bishop is White's best. Others are less troubling:

a) 6 ♗b5 a6 7 ♗xc6+ bxc6 is not an effective continuation for White, e.g. 8 h3 ♗h5 9 g4 ♗g6 10 ♘d2 d5 11 e5 ♘d7 (the black light-squared bishop has a wonderful diagonal to operate on) 12 ♘b3 (White is probably hoping to take the initiative on the queenside with ♘a5, but Black takes action first) 12...h5 (Black takes the opportunity to disrupt White's kingside before he can build up a threatening position with f4) 13 ♖f1 ♕h4 (now if White defends his h-pawn with 14 ♕f3 Black can reply 14...♗xc2) 14 g5 ♕xh3 15 ♕d2 ♕f3 16 ♘e2 ♕f5 17 c3 a5 18 ♘f4 c5 19 ♘xg6 ♕xg6 20 f4 cxd4 21 ♘xd4 ♕e4 and

Black won easily, Jukic-Klinger, Vienna 1991.

b) 6 ♕d2 is not really to the point as White should be concentrating on building up an initiative on the light squares, e.g. 6...d5 7 e5 ♘d7 8 ♗e2 ♗e7 9 h3 ♗h5 10 0-0 0-0 11 ♘e1 ♗xe2 12 ♘xe2 f6 (Black has achieved a French Defence structure without being hampered by a constricted queen's bishop) 13 ♘f4 ♕e8 14 c3 (one point of Black's play is that 14 ♘xe6 ♗b4 15 c3 ♕xe6 16 cxb4 fxe5 leaves him with an excellent position) 14...♕f7 15 exf6 ♘xf6 16 ♘f3 ♘e4 17 ♕d1 ♗d6 18 ♘d3 ♕f5 19 ♘h4 ♕f6 20 ♕g4 ♖ae8 21 ♘f3 ♖f7 22 ♖ae1 ♖ef8 23 ♗c1 a5 with an equal game, Almasi-Klinger, Balatonbereny 1993.

6 ♗e2 is examined in game 27.

**6  ...  ♗h5**

**7  ♗b5**

This pin is how White used to handle this variation but in fact line 'b' of the alternatives below is more testing.

a) 7 ♕e2

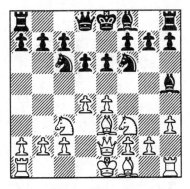

7...d5 8 g4 ♗g6 9 exd5 ♘xd5 10 a3 (White is obliged to waste this tempo as Black's powerful bishop on g6 makes ...♘db4 a strong threat) 10...h5 11 ♘xd5 ♕xd5 12 ♗g2 hxg4 13 hxg4 ♖xh1+ 14 ♗xh1 0-0-0

(Black already stands slightly better) 15 ♗g2 ♗e7 (White would like to bring his king to the queenside but 16 0-0-0 will be met by 16...♕a2) 16 c4 ♕a5+ 17 ♔f1 ♕a4 18 ♔g1

(White has brought his king to safety but his position, especially the central pawns, remains uncomfortably exposed) 18...♗f6 19 ♖d1 ♗c2 20 ♖c1 ♗e4 21 g5 ♗e7 22 ♖c3 (White has just managed to hold the centre together but now Black turns his attention to the kingside) 22...♕a5 23 ♘e5 (this leads to an endgame a pawn down, but the alternative 23 b4 ♕f5 24 ♘h4 ♕h7 25 ♕g4 ♗xg2 26 ♘xg2 ♖h8 was worse) 23...♗xg2 24 ♔xg2 ♘xe5 25 dxe5 ♕xe5 26 ♕f3 ♕f5 27 ♕xf5 exf5 28 ♖c1 ♖d3 and Black won, Gi. Hernandez-Miles, Seville 1994.

b) 7 d5 is a dangerous move for Black who now has two possibilities:

a) 7...♘e7 and now:

a1) 8 ♗b5+ c6 9 dxc6 bxc6 (this is a natural recapture but it leaves Black with trouble coordinating his forces, so he should consider 9...♘xc6 which leaves White with only a small edge after 10 ♕e2 ♗e7) 10 ♗a4 ♕c7 (Black is hoping to get developed with ...♘c8 and ...♗e7, but this is all very slow and White cuts across this plan with a series of active moves) 11 ♕e2! ♘d7 12 g4 ♗g6 13 0-0-0

13...e5 (examples of Black's problems can be seen from the variations: 13...d5 14 exd5 cxd5 15 ♘xd5! exd5 16 ♖xd5 ♘xd5 17 ♗b6+ ♗e7 18 ♗xc7 ♘xc7 19 ♖d1 and 13...0-0-0 14 ♕a6+ ♔b8 15 ♖xd6 ♕xd6 16 ♘b5 and White wins in both cases) 14 ♕c4 (an earlier game, Apicella-David, Linares 1995, finished abruptly after 14 ♘h4!? ♘c8? 15 ♕c4 ♘c5 16 ♗xc5 dxc5 17 ♕d5 1-0) 14...♖c8 15 ♘h4 ♘b6 16 ♗xb6 axb6 17 ♖d3 (White prepares a powerful exchange sacrifice) 17...d5 18 exd5 ♗xd3 19 ♕xd3 ♖d8 20 ♖d1 g6 21 d6 ♗h6+ 22 ♔b1 ♕b8 23 ♘e4 b5 24 ♘f6+ ♔f8 25 dxe7+ ♔xe7 26 ♘d7! bxa4 27 ♘f5+! gxf5 28 ♕a3+

♔e6 29 gxf5+ ♔xf5 30 ♕f3+ 1-0 Illescas-Miles, Linares 1995.

a2) 8 ♗e2

allows Black to complete his development without trouble: 8...exd5 9 exd5 ♗xf3 10 ♗xf3 ♘f5 11 ♗g5 ♗e7 12 0-0 0-0 13 ♖e1 ♘d7 (Black frees himself with exchanges) 14 ♗xe7 ♘xe7 15 ♕d2 ♘g6 (the position is equal) 16 g3 ♕f6 17 ♗g2 ♖ae8 18 b3?! (weakening the long diagonal like this creates tactical opportunities for Black) 18...h5! (this advance provokes White into weakening his kingside) 19 h4 ♘ge5 20 f4 ♘g4 21 ♘e4 ♕g6 22 ♘g5 ♘df6 23 a4 ♕f5 24 ♗f3 c6 and Black has an edge, Klovans-Miles, Groningen 1992.

b) 7...exd5 8 exd5 ♘e5 (this is best as 8...♗xf3 9 ♕xf3 ♘e5 10 ♕e2 gives White a free hand to develop a kingside initiative, e.g. 10...a6 11 0-0-0 ♗e7 12 f4 ♘g6 13 g4 ♘d7 14 g5 0-0 15 h4 ♖e8 16 h5 ♘gf8 17 ♕d2 c5

18 dxc6 bxc6 19 h6 g6 20 ♘e4 with powerful play, Golubev-Markowski, Biel 1995) 9 g4

9...♗g6 (this is preferable to 9...♘xf3+ 10 ♕xf3 ♗g6 11 0-0-0 a6 12 ♗d4 ♗e7 13 ♕e2 0-0 14 f4 h6 15 f5 ♗h7 16 ♕f3 ♖e8 17 ♔b1 when Black is left with an entombed bishop on h7 Spraggett-Mohr, Ubeda 1996) 10 ♗b5+ (10 ♘xe5 dxe5 solves many of Black's problems by allowing him to develop his king's bishop actively while 10 ♘d4 is well met by 10...c5 11 ♗b5+ ♘fd7) 10...♘ed7 11 ♕e2 ♗e7 12 0-0-0 a6 13 ♗d3 ♗xd3 14 ♖xd3 0-0 15 ♘d4 ♘c5 16 ♖dd1 ♖e8 and the exchange of bishops has eased the congestion in Black's position and he went on to win in 40 moves, I.V. Ivanov-Nesterov, Moscow 1995. Black has avoided weakening his kingside and will consolidate with ...♗f8. He can then begin counterplay on the queenside with ...b5. This is clearly the best way for Black to

handle the variation which starts with 7...exd5.

| 7 | ... | a6 |
| 8 | ♗a4 | |

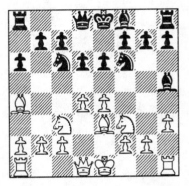

| 8 | ... | ♘d7 |

Not, of course 8...b5 9 ♘xb5 axb5 10 ♗xb5 ♕d7 11 d5 and White wins.

| 9 | d5 | ♘a5 |
| 10 | ♕e2 | b5 |

Once again White has been thrown on his own resources in the opening and the absence of theoretical guidance means that Black has swiftly achieved a fully playable position.

| 11 | ♗b3 | e5 |
| 12 | a3 | |

This looks like a terrible strategic concession, but White hopes to gain compensation on the open c-file.

| 12 | ... | ♘xb3 |
| 13 | cxb3 | ♗e7 |
| 14 | b4 | 0-0 |
| 15 | g4 | |

White was clearly worried by the prospect of ...f5, liberating Black's position but now

White's whole position is beginning to look like a Swiss cheese with holes all over the place.

| 21 | ♘d5 | ♕b7 |
| 22 | axb5 | axb5 |
| 23 | 0-0 | ♗d8 |
| 24 | ♖fc1 | f5 |

| 15 | ... | ♗g6 |
| 16 | ♘d2 | ♘b6 |
| 17 | b3 | ♖c8 |
| 18 | a4 | c6 |

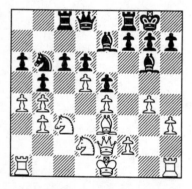

Paradoxically, Black is the first to utilise the open c-file.

| 19 | dxc6 | ♖xc6 |
| 20 | ♗xb6 | |

White is hoping to gain control of d5 in order to stabilise the situation.

| 20 | ... | ♕xb6 |

A superb coup from Miles which must have come as a terrible shock to his opponent. Black speculates on being able to undermine White's apparently impregnable knight on the d5-square.

| 25 | exf5 | |

25 gxf5 meets with the same response.

| 25 | ... | ♗xf5 |

Now 26 gxf5 ♖xc1 27 ♕xd5 would leave White with weak pawns everywhere.

| 26 | ♖xc6 | ♕xc6 |
| 27 | ♕f3 | |

Threatening ♘e7+ so Black must defend his queen.

| 27 | ... | ♗d7 |
| 28 | ♕e4 | ♔h8 |
| 29 | ♖d1 | ♕a8 |

A marvellous retreat, which prepares to bring Black's bishops into scything action against White's king.

| 30 | ♘f1 | ♗c6 |
| 31 | ♘fe3 | ♖f4 |
| 32 | ♕c2 | ♖d4 |

With a few deft strokes Black has forced the win of material. White now loses a piece.

| 33 | ♖c1 | ♗xd5 |
| 34 | ♕c8 | |

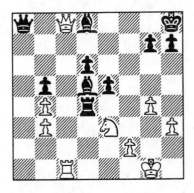

A final throw, which Black refutes brilliantly.

| 34 | ... | ♖c4 |

A wonderful riposte, which blocks the connection between White's pieces and banishes any prospect of counterplay. If now 35 ♕xa8 Black wins with the

intermezzo 35...♖xc1+.

| 35 | ♖xc4 | bxc4 |
| 36 | ♕d7 | ♕a1+ |
| 37 | ♘f1 | cxb3 |
| 38 | ♕xd6 | |

Equally, if 38 ♕xd8+ then 38...♗g8 is a simple win.

| 38 | ... | ♗g8 |
| | **0-1** | |

### Game 26
### Doric-Mestrovic
*Bled 1996*

| 1 | e4 | ♘c6 |
| 2 | ♘f3 | d6 |
| 3 | d4 | ♘f6 |
| 4 | ♘c3 | ♗g4 |
| 5 | ♗e3 | |

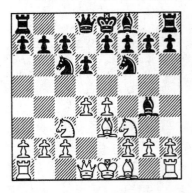

| 5 | ... | e5 |

This leads to positions where Black is a little cramped but has a very solid position and chances for long term counterplay. It is thus a good choice against an opponent who is impatient and may over-extend himself.

Black has two alternatives

here which both lead to complex play:

a) 5...a6 eliminates the problem of a white bishop check on b5 but is a little slow. Play can continue 6 h3 ♗h5

7 d5 (quiet development with 7 ♗e2 is not dangerous for Black, e.g. 7...e6 8 0-0 d5 9 exd5 ♘xd5 10 ♘xd5 exd5 11 ♘e5 ♗xe2 12 ♕xe2 ♘xe5 13 ♗f4 ♗e7 14 ♗xe5 0-0 15 ♕g4 f6 16 ♗f4 ♕c8 17 ♖fe1 ♕xg4 18 hxg4 ♔f7 19 ♖e3 c6 with a completely equal position, Luther-Miles, Hastings 1995/6) and now:

a1) 7...♘b8 (Miles has had no joy with the active 7...♗xf3 - see note 'a2' - so Black should consider this simple knight retreat) 8 a4 ♗xf3 9 ♕xf3 g6 10 ♕d1 ♗g7 11 ♗e2 0-0 12 0-0 c6 (Black has a type of position familiar from the Pirc Defence) 13 a5 ♘bd7 14 f4 ♕b8 (Black delays exchanging on d5 as, compared with Garcia-Miles below, this makes it more diffi-

cult for White to form a plan) 15 ♖a3 ♕c7 16 ♕d3 ♖fe8 17 g4 cxd5 (now that White has exposed his king Black feels more comfortable about opening the centre) 18 exd5 e6 19 dxe6 ♖xe6 20 g5 ♖ae8 21 ♗d4 ♘e4 22 ♗xg7 ♔xg7 23 ♕d4+ ♔g8 24 ♗g4 ♘xc3 25 ♖xc3 ♕xa5 26 ♗xe6 ♖xe6 27 ♖e3 ♖xe3 28 ♕xe3 ♕f5 (the open white king makes it very difficult for him to realise the advantage of the exchange) 29 ♕d3 ♕e6 30 b4 h6 31 gxh6 ♔h7 32 f5 ♕e7 33 ♕g3 ♔xh6 34 h4 ♘e5 35 ♕f4+ ♔h7 36 ♕g5 ♕c7 37 fxg6+ fxg6 38 h5 ♕xc2 39 ♕e7+ ♔h6 40 ♕xd6 ♕e4 41 hxg6 ♕g4+ ½-½ Yagupov-Hodgson, Linares 1996.

a2) 7...♗xf3 and now:

a21) 8 ♕xf3 ♘e5 9 ♕d1 c6 10 f4 ♘ed7 11 ♗e2 cxd5 (it may be better to avoid this exchange for the moment - see Yagupov-Hodgson above) 12 exd5 g6 13 ♕d2 ♗g7 14 a4 ♕a5 15 0-0 0-0 16 ♖a3 ♖ac8 (Black is struggling to create play while White has a plan to advance on the queenside) 17 ♖d1 ♘c5 18 ♗f3 ♘cd7 19 ♖b1 ♖c4 20 ♗e2 ♖cc8 21 b4 ♕c7 22 a5 e5 23 dxe6 fxe6 24 b5 ♘c5 25 bxa6 bxa6 26 ♖b6 and White has a clear advantage, Gi. Garcia-Miles, Wijk aan Zee 1996.

a22) 8 gxf3 ♘b8 9 f4 c6 (this opens up the position to White's advantage so Black would be better advised to try to complete his development with 9...e6 or 9...g6) 10 ♗g2 ♕c7 11 ♕d4 cxd5 12 ♘xd5 ♘xd5 13 exd5 ♘d7 14 c4 ♘f6 15 ♖c1 g6 16 c5 dxc5 17 ♖xc5 ♕d6 18 ♕a4+ ♘d7 19 ♖c6!

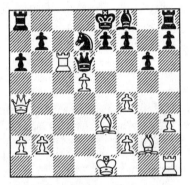

19...♕b8 (19...bxc6 20 dxc6 ♖c8 21 ♕xa6 is hopeless for Black) 20 ♖b6 ♕c8 21 0-0 ♖b8 22 ♖c1 ♕d8 23 d6 ♗g7 24 ♖xb7 ♖xb7 25 ♗xb7 0-0 1-0 Onishchuk-Miles, Wijk aan Zee 1996.

b) 5...g6 is playable. Black is again angling for a Pirc Defence but White gains free development for his pieces, e.g. 6 h3 ♗xf3 7 ♕xf3 ♗g7 8 ♗b5 (this is a rather feeble continuation and more to the point is 8 0-0-0 0-0 9 g4 e5 10 dxe5 ♘xe5 11 ♕g2 a6 12 g5 and White obtains good attacking chances, Hübner-Wockenfuss, Bundesliga 1986) 8...0-0 9 0-0 ♘d7 10 ♖ad1 e5 11 ♗xc6 bxc6 12 dxe5 ♘xe5 13 ♕e2 ♕b8 14 b3 ♕b4

15 ♗d2 ♖fe8 16 ♖fe1 ♘d7 and the position is about equal, Kornasiewicz-Angelov, Warsaw 1989.

**6   ♗b5**

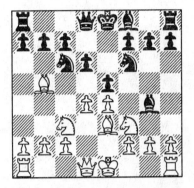

This is the most dynamic continuation for White. Others:

a) The immediate 6 d5 is less worrying, e.g. 6...♘e7 7 ♗e2 (7 h3 ♗d7 8 a4 ♘g6 9 a5 a6 10 g3 ♗e7 11 ♘h2 0-0 12 h4 ♕c8 13 ♗e2 ♗d8 14 ♗g5 ♘e8 15 ♗g4 ♗xg5 16 ♗xd7 ♕xd7 17 hxg5 f6 18 ♘f3 ♕g4 19 gxf6 ♘xf6 20 ♘d2 ♕d7 21 ♕e2 ♖f7 22 ♘d1 ♘e7 23 ♘e3 ♖af8 24 f3 and the exchange of two pairs of minor pieces has helped Black to activate his position and obtain equal chances, Damljanovic-Mestrovic, Yugoslavia 1989) 7...♘g6 8 ♘d2 ♗d7 (although Black wants, in principle, to exchange pieces, this is a good piece and so he prefers, for the moment at least, to retreat it) 9 ♘c4 ♗e7 10 a4 0-0 11 0-0 h6 12 a5 a6 13 b4 ♘h7 14 ♗g4 ♗g5

(the plan to exchange dark-squared bishops with ...♗g5 is a typical one for this variation) 15 ♖b1 ♘e7 16 ♗xd7 ♕xd7 17 b5 f5 18 bxa6 bxa6 19 f3 ♗xe3+ 20 ♘xe3 ♘f6 21 ♕d3 g6 22 ♖b7 f4 23 ♘c4 ♖fb8 24 ♖bb1 g5 25 ♘d2 ♖xb1 26 ♖xb1 g4 and Black had excellent king-side counterplay in the game Wedberg-Mestrovic, Biel 1990.

b) 6 ♗e2 ♗e7 7 0-0 0-0 8 d5 ♘b8 9 ♘e1 ♗c8 (Black carefully leaves the d7-square free for use by his knights) 10 f4 exf4 11 ♗xf4 ♘fd7 12 ♘f3 ♗f6 13 ♕d2 ♕e7 (although White has a big lead in development, Black has very strong control over the central dark squares) 14 ♘d4 ♘e5 15 ♘f5 (this is playing into Black's hands and White would do much better to keep pieces on the board with a simple move such as 15 ♖ae1) 15...♗xf5 16 exf5 ♘ed7 (this is an excellent regrouping by Black - the natural 16...♘bd7 would leave his

knights very statically positioned) 17 ♖ae1 ♗e5 18 ♗g5 ♘f6 19 ♗d3 ♘bd7 20 ♔h1 ♖fe8 21 ♘e4 ♘xe4 22 ♖xe4 f6 23 ♗h4 ♕f7 24 b4 (24 b3 is preferable to this weakening move) 24...a5 25 a3 axb4 26 axb4 ♖a3 27 ♕e2 ♖ea8 28 ♗c4 ♘b6 29 ♗b3 ♘xd5 30 ♕c4 c6 and Black went on to win in the game Krieger-Mestrovic, Werfen 1993.

6 ... ♘d7
7 d5

7 ... ♘cb8
Black side-steps the cunning trap 7...♘e7? 8 ♘xe5! ♗xd1 9 ♗xd7+ ♕xd7 10 ♘xd7 ♗xc2 11 ♘xf8 ♗d3 12 0-0-0 ♗a6 13 ♘xh7 and White emerges a pawn ahead in the endgame.

Black's play (...♘fd7 and ...♘cb8) seems very retrograde but with a blocked position this is not of great importance. Furthermore, if White wants to play either of the natural advances c4 or f4, he will have some regrouping to do himself.

**8    ♗e2**

An alternative way for White to deploy his pieces is 8 ♕d2 ♗e7 9 0-0-0 0-0 10 ♖dg1 ♘f6 11 ♘e1 c5 12 f3 a6 13 ♗f1 ♗c8 14 g4 b5 15 h4 ♘e8 Beshukov-Mestrovic, Ljubljana 1994.

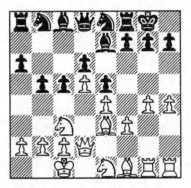

White has a space advantage and attacking prospects on the kingside. However, Black has been careful not to weaken himself and so it will take White a long time to force a breakthrough on the kingside. Meanwhile Black will be able to generate queenside play. This is a typical position arising from 5...e5. White has an edge but the battle has only just begun.

**8    ...       ♗e7**
**9    ♕d2      ♘f6**

In an earlier game Mestrovic, an expert in this variation, unnecessarily weakened his kingside with 9...h6?! and quickly paid the penalty: 10 0-0-0 ♗xf3 11 gxf3! (Black was no doubt anticipating 11 ♗xf3 ♗g5 when

he has solved his opening problems) 11...a6 (following 11...♗g5 White has the pleasant choice between 12 ♗xg5 ♕xg5 13 ♕xg5 hxg5 14 ♖dg1 f6 15 h4 and 12 f4 exf4 13 ♗xf4 ♗xf4 14 ♕xf4) 12 f4 exf4 13 ♗xf4 ♗g5 14 ♗xg5 ♕xg5 (after 14...hxg5 White gains a big advantage with the same idea as in the game, viz. 15 ♖dg1 f6 16 h4) 15 ♕xg5 hxg5 16 ♖dg1 f6 17 h4 0-0 18 ♗g4! g6 19 h5

(White now gains a winning attack on the kingside despite the absence of queens) 19...♘e5 20 hxg6 ♘xg4 (20...♘xg6 21 ♗f5 ♔g7 22 f4 ♘xf4 23 ♖h7+ ♔g8 24 ♖gh1 and the black position has been completely invaded) 21 ♖xg4 ♘d7 22 f4 ♖ae8 23 ♖h7 f5 24 ♖xg5 ♘f6 25 ♖h1 ♔g7 26 ♖xf5 1-0 Sveshnikov-Mestrovic, Ljubljana 1994.

**10    h3**

After 10 0-0-0 ♗xf3 11 ♗xf3 c5 12 g4 a6 13 ♘e2 ♕d7 14 g5

♘g4 15 ♗xg4 ♕xg4 the exchange of pieces has eased Black's cramp. The game Pavasovic-Mestrovic, Nova Gorica 1996 continued 16 f4 ♘d7 17 ♖hg1 ♕h4 18 ♘g3 exf4 19 ♗xf4 g6 20 ♔b1 0-0 21 ♕e3 ♖ae8 22 ♖df1 ½-½.

| 10 | ... | ♗h5 |

10...♗xf3 is, of course, perfectly playable but Mestrovic has a different idea in mind.

| 11 | ♕d3 | 0-0 |
| 12 | g4 | ♗g6 |

This bishop regrouping seems strange but Black is hoping to undermine the white centre with ...c6. The opposition of the black bishop and white queen will make this thrust particularly strong.

| 13 | h4 |

Not 13 ♘h4?, which fails to the standard tactic 13...♗xe4 14 ♘xe4 ♘xe4.

White is hoping to use the black bishop on g6 as a target for his kingside advance but the black position proves sufficiently resilient to cope with this attack.

| 13 | ... | h5 |
| 14 | g5 |

White closes the position, speculating on the long-term weakness of the black h-pawn. An alternative strategy was to keep the position on the kingside open with 14 gxh5.

| 14 | ... | ♘fd7 |
| 15 | 0-0-0 | ♘a6 |
| 16 | ♘d2 | ♘ac5 |
| 17 | ♗xc5 | ♘xc5 |
| 18 | ♕e3 |

Given time White will now bring his knight on d2 round to g3 and win the black h-pawn. However, by opening the centre Black generates sufficient counterplay to avoid this.

| 18 | ... | c6 |
| 19 | ♘f1 | cxd5 |
| 20 | ♖xd5 |

Of course 20 ♘xd5 leaves the e-pawn *en prise*, but another way for White to play was 20 exd5 ♕a5 (20...f5 21 gxf6 ♗xf6 is dangerous for Black as lines on the kingside are opened) 21 ♞g3 (Black has very good piece play on the queenside, which makes it difficult for White to carry out his plan, e.g. 21 ♔b1 ♖ac8 22 ♞g3 ♞a4 and Black is very active) 21...♞a4 22 ♞xa4 ♕xa4 23 ♖b3 ♕xb3 24 axb3 f6 and Black has the more active position in the endgame.

| 20 | ... | ♞e6 |
|----|------|------|
| 21 | ♞g3 | ♞f4 |
| 22 | ♖dd1 | f6 |
| 23 | ♞d5 | fxg5 |
| 24 | ♞xe7+ | ♕xe7 |
| 25 | hxg5 | |

| 25 | ... | ♕f7? |

After this move White is able to co-ordinate his position. Black should have continued his dynamic play with 25...♞xe2+! 26 ♞xe2 (26 ♕xe2 ♕xg5+ 27 ♔b1 h4 is very good for Black) 26...♕f7 (hitting a2 and f2) 27 ♞c3 ♕xf2 28 ♕xf2 ♖xf2 29 ♖xd6 ♔h7 and the outside passed h-pawn should guarantee Black a good endgame.

The failure to exchange with

25...♞xe2+ is a very common type of mistake. The black knight is a much better piece than the white bishop and so exchanging it seems illogical. However, this is a case where the tactical considerations (i.e. Black is able to continue his initiative) outweigh the positional ones (i.e. the black knight is better than the black bishop).

| 26 | ♔b1 | ♖ac8 |

If Black tries to get back into the endgame in the last note with 26...♞xe2 White can improve with 27 ♕xe2 ♕xf2 28 ♕xf2 ♖xf2 29 ♖xd6 and the vulnerability of the h-pawn will make it difficult for Black to play for the advantage.

| 27 | ♗b5? | |

Now everything is again okay for Black. White should have played 27 ♖xd6 and if 27...h4 28 ♞f5 ♗xf5 29 exf5 ♞xe2 (29...♕xf5 30 ♕b3+ ♕f7 31 ♕xf7+ ♖xf7 32 ♗g4 and White is much better) 30 ♕xe2 ♕xf5 31 ♖xh4 ♕xf2 32 ♕xf2 ♖xf2 with a draw in prospect.

| 27 | ... | h4 |

This pawn cannot be captured (28 ♖xh4 ♞g2) and now the white position collapses.

| 28 | ♞e2 | ♞g2 |
|----|------|------|
| 29 | ♕b3 | ♕xb3 |
| 30 | axb3 | ♖xf2 |
| 31 | ♞c3 | ♖d8 |

Black is a pawn ahead and the passed h-pawn is very strong. The game is effectively decided.

| 32 | ♗c4+ | ♗f7 |
| 33 | ♖df1 | ♖f4 |
| 34 | ♗xf7+ | ♔xf7 |
| 35 | ♘d5 | ♖xf1+ |
| 36 | ♖xf1+ | ♔g6 |
| 37 | ♖f5 | ♔h5 |
| | 0-1 | |

### Game 27
### Rodriguez-Miles
*Palma de Mallorca 1989*

| 1 | e4 | ♘c6 |
| 2 | ♘f3 | d6 |
| 3 | d4 | ♘f6 |
| 4 | ♘c3 | ♗g4 |
| 5 | ♗e3 | e6 |
| 6 | ♗e2 | ♗e7 |
| 7 | 0-0 | |

7 ♕d2 a6 8 d5 exd5 9 exd5 ♗xf3 10 gxf3 (White tries this recapture in a number of examples in this section; the idea is to save time and utilise the open g-file for attacking purposes) 10...♘e5 11 f4 ♘ed7 12 0-0-0 0-0 13 ♖hg1 c5 14 ♖g2 ♖e8 15 ♖dg1 ♗f8 (Black is careful to avoid, for the moment at least,

the weakening ...g6) 16 ♗f3 ♕a5 17 ♔b1 ♔h8 18 ♗g4 ♖ad8 19 ♕d3 b5 20 ♗xd7 ♖xd7 21 ♕f5 ♕d8 22 ♘e2 g6 23 ♕d3 ♗g7 24 f5 ♖e5 25 fxg6 hxg6 26 ♘f4 ♕a8 27 ♖g5 ♖de7 28 h4 with a complex position, Lyrberg-Malaniuk, Lyngby 1991.

| 7 | ... | 0-0 |

| 8 | ♖e1 | |

With 8 ♘d2 White hopes to mount a kingside attack by freeing a path for his f-pawn to advance, e.g. 8...♗xe2 9 ♕xe2 d5 10 e5 ♘d7 11 f4 f5 (Black cuts across White's immediate plans) 12 exf6 ♗xf6 13 ♘f3 ♕e7 14 ♕d2 ♖ae8 15 ♖ae1 ♕b4 16 b3 ♘b6 (Black regroups his knight to d6 in order to keep an eye on the important central light squares e4 and f5) 17 ♖e2 ♘c8 18 ♕d3 ♘d6 19 ♘b1 a6 20 c3 ♕b5 21 ♕c2 ♘e7 22 a4 ♕c6 23 ♘bd2 ♘df5 24 ♕d3 ♕d6 25 ♗f2 ♕xf4 26 ♖xe6 ♘g6 27 ♖xe8 ♖xe8 28 ♖e1 ♖xe1+ 29 ♘xe1 c6 with an equal endgame, Adams-Miles,

Intel Grand Prix, London 1995.

**8 ... d5**

Black's plan in this variation is to head for a French Defence structure but with his queen's bishop outside the pawn chain.

**9 h3**

9 exd5 would lead to a completely equal position. White must keep the tension to have any hope of obtaining the advantage.

**9 ... ♗h5**

**10 e5 ②d7**

Also possible is 10...②e4 11 ②xe4 dxe4 12 ②h2 ♗g6 with an unclear position.

| **11** | **♕d2** | **②b6** |
| **12** | **b3** | **♗g6** |
| **13** | **♗d3** | **♕d7** |
| **14** | **②e2** | **②b4** |
| **15** | **♗xg6** | **fxg6** |

In principle, such recaptures should be made towards the centre, i.e. 15...hxg6. Here, however, Black frees his position considerably be playing ...fxg6 and the open f-file proves to be an excellent route

for his counterplay.

**16 c3 ②a6**

Black is now preparing the standard thrust ...c5. The earlier piece exchange has left White with a passive bishop, which he now tries to exchange.

**17 ♗g5 ♗a3**

White's bishop is slightly hampering his other pieces and so Black declines to allow the exchange.

**18 ♕c2**

White is insistent. He clears the c1-square in order to be able to offer the bishop exchange once again.

**18 ... ♖ac8**

**19 b4**

Suddenly White completely changes his plan. The logical follow-up to his previous play would have been 19 ♗c1 ♗e7 20 ♗g5 but then Black continues 20...♗xg5 21 ②xg5 c5 and the opposition of the white queen and black rook on the c-file allows Black to gain more time.

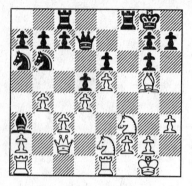

**19   ...      ♖xf3!**

This is a very important sacrifice for Black. White's last move cut off the black bishop at the expense of acquiring serious weaknesses on the queenside, particularly, the c4-square. The best way for White to cover this weakness is by playing ♞d2 and so Black immediately eliminates this knight. Note that the other knight, on e2, is four moves away from being able to attack the c4-square.

**20   gxf3**

Black has excellent compensation for the exchange as White has unpleasant weaknesses on both sides of the board. Black's knight on a6 and his bishop on a3 are temporarily out of play, but the closed nature of the position means that White is unable to co-ordinate his forces successfully before Black can regroup.

| 20 | ... | ♖f8 |
| 21 | ♔g2 | ♕f7 |
| 22 | ♕d3 | ♞c4 |

**23   ♗c1**

It may seem strange to exchange off Black's wandering bishop on a3, but this piece was not going to be out of play for ever (Black will play ...a5 one day). Meanwhile White wants to create threats by advancing on the kingside with h4 and f4 and his own bishop is in the way.

| 23 | ... | ♗xc1 |
| 24 | ♖axc1 | ♞b8 |

24...g5!? was an interesting alternative. Black is planning ...♞a6-b8-c6-e7-g6 but there is a danger that White may be able to co-ordinate himself in order to be able to play h4 before Black completes his regrouping. After 24...g5!?, 25 h4?! immediately is not advisable on account of 25...g4.

| 25 | h4 | ♞c6 |
| 26 | f4 | ♞e7 |
| 27 | ♖h1 | ♞f5 |
| 28 | ♖h3 | |

The black knights have wonderful outposts and if White

tries to eliminate one of them
with 28 ♘g3 Black can continue 28...♕e7 29 ♘xf5 ♖xf5
and the white f-pawn is very
vulnerable.

| 28 | ... | ♕e7 |
| 29 | ♖ch1 | |

| 29 | ... | a5! |

White is preparing to create
threats on the kingside with h5
and so Black opens a line on the
queenside to activate his own
rook.

| 30 | bxa5 | ♖a8 |
| 31 | ♘g3 | ♖xa5 |
| 32 | h5 | ♕f7! |

Black's plan is to meet 33
hxg6 with 33...♕xg6. White can
then capture on h7 and even
check on h8, but the black king
will run away to f7 and maybe
e7, where it will be difficult to
get at. Meanwhile the white
king will come under a heavy
attack from the black pieces.

| 33 | ♕b1 | b6 |
| 34 | hxg6 | |

Not 34 ♘xf5 gxf5 when
White has no possibility of

breaking through anywhere and
Black has all the play.

| 34 | ... | ♕xg6 |
| 35 | ♖xh7 | |

| 35 | ... | ♔f7!! |

Miles commences a brilliant
king march which decides the
game in his favour. He has re-
alised that his king will be
safely placed on d7 and that
immediate attacking attempts
do not succeed, e.g. 35...♘ce3+
36 ♔g1 ♕g4 (36...♘h4 hoping
for 37 ♕xg6 ♘f3 mate, is a nice
try but unfortunately fails to 37
♖h8+! and White wins) 37
♖h8+ ♔f7 38 ♕b4 and the
threats to invade on f8 leave
Black with a lost position, e.g.
38...♘xg3 39 ♕f8+ ♔g6 40
♖1h6+ gxh6 41 ♖xh6 mate.

| 36 | ♖7h5 | |

The main point of Black's
play is revealed after 36 ♖h8
♔e7!! (36...♘ce3+ 37 ♔g1 fails
as in the previous note) 37 ♖c8
after (37 ♕b4+ ♔d7 Black's
king is safe and his own attack
will quickly be decisive)

37...♘ce3+ 38 ♔g1 ♘h4!!

| 40 | ♔h1 | ♛f3+ |
| 41 | ♔g1 | ♛g4+ |

(now this really does work)
39 ♛b4+ (39 ♛xg6 ♘f3 mate)
39...c5 winning. White therefore brings his rook back to ful-
fil a defensive role.

| 36 | ... | ♘ce3+! |
| 37 | ♔g1 | ♛g4 |

| 38 | ♖1h2 |

Others:

a) 38 ♖g5 ♛xf4 winning.

b) 38 ♖1h3 ♘xg3 39 ♖xg3
♛xh5 40 fxe3 ♖a8 and ...♖h8 is
coming.

| 38 | ... | ♘xg3 |
| 39 | fxg3 | ♛xg3+ |

**42  ♔f2?**

After this White is lost. He
should have played 42 ♔h1 ♖b5
43 ♛c1 (forced) 43...♛g6 44 f5
and now Black can choose between 44...exf5, planning ...f4
and 44...♘xf5 45 ♖g5 ♖b1!
with a clear plus in either case.

| 42 | ... | ♘d1+ |
| 43 | ♔f1 | ♘e3+ |
| 44 | ♔f2 | ♘d1+ |
| 45 | ♔f1 | ♛f3+ |
| 46 | ♔g1 | ♛e3+ |
| 47 | ♔f1 | ♘xc3 |

The black attack is now too hot for White to handle.

| | | |
|---|---|---|
| 48 | ♕e1 | ♕d3+ |
| 49 | ♔g1 | ♖b5 |
| 50 | ♖5h3 | |

Or 50 ♖d2 ♕g6+ 51 ♖g5 ♖b1 52 ♖xg6 ♖xe1+ 53 ♔f2 ♖d1 54 ♖c2 ♔xg6 55 ♖xc3 ♖xd4 56 ♖xc7 ♖xf4+ and Black wins.

| | | |
|---|---|---|
| 50 | ... | ♕xd4+ |
| 51 | ♔g2 | ♖b2+ |
| 52 | ♔f3 | ♕d3+ |
| 53 | ♔g4 | ♕f5+ |
| 54 | ♔f3 | ♘e2 |
| | **0-1** | |

**Game 28**
**Almasi-Miles**
*Groningen 1994*

| | | |
|---|---|---|
| 1 | e4 | ♘c6 |
| 2 | ♘f3 | d6 |
| 3 | d4 | ♘f6 |
| 4 | ♘c3 | ♗g4 |
| 5 | ♗e2 | e6 |
| 6 | h3 | |

White is planning to advance with d5 and this can also be played immediately, e.g. 6 d5

a) 8 gxf3!? ♘e5 9 ♗e3 ♗e7 10 ♕d2 0-0 11 0-0-0 c5 12 ♖dg1 ♘e8 13 f4 ♘d7 14 ♘e4 a6 15 f5?! (this allows Black to consolidate his position on the kingside and so White should prefer instead 15 h4, which keeps his kingside build-up flexible) 15...♘df6 16 ♘g5?! ♕d7 17 ♕d3 ♕b5! (Black cleverly provokes White into advancing his queenside pawns to provide targets) 18 c4 ♕a4 19 ♔b1 b5 20 ♕b3 ♕xb3 21 axb3 ♘c7 and Black has a small edge in the endgame, Timoshenko-Miles, Moscow 1990.

b) 8 ♗xf3 ♘e5 9 ♗e2 ♗e7 10 ♗e3 (unless White is prepared to unbalance the position by committing his king to the queenside, he is unlikely to obtain an advantage, e.g. 10 0-0 0-0 11 ♗e3 ♘fd7 12 ♕d2 ♘g6 13 ♘b5 ♗f6 14 ♘d4 ♖e8 15 c3 ♘e7 16 c4 ♗xd4 17 ♗xd4 ♘f5 18 ♗c3 ♘c5 and Black has a comfortable game, Grünfeld-

Miles, Biel 1995) 10...0-0 11 f4 ♘ed7 12 ♕d2 ♘c5 13 ♗f3 ♕d7 (this leaves Black cramped and a better plan is 13...♖e8 when Black can follow up with ...♗f8 and the d7-square is left free for the f6-knight to use, e.g. 13...♖e8 14 0-0-0 ♗f8 and Black has the options of bringing a knight to e4 or taking the initiative on the queenside with ...a6 and ...b5) 14 0-0-0 ♖ae8 15 ♗d4 ♗d8 16 ♖he1 ♖xe1 17 ♖xe1 ♖e8 18 g4 ♖xe1+ 19 ♕xe1 h6 20 h3 a6 21 ♕e3 ♕e7 22 ♕xe7 ♗xe7 23 b4 and White has a small advantage in the endgame, Dlugy-Miles, USA Ch 1989.

| 6  | ...  | ♗h5  |
|----|------|------|
| 7  | d5   | exd5 |
| 8  | exd5 | ♗xf3 |
| 9  | ♗xf3 | ♘e5  |
| 10 | ♗e2  | ♗e7  |

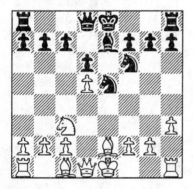

**11    0-0**

11 f4 ♘g6 12 0-0 0-0 13 ♗d3 c5 14 ♕f3 a6 15 a4 ♘e8 16 g3 ♘c7 17 h4 (as White never gets round to playing h5, this plan

only serves to weaken his king-side) 17...♗f6 18 ♗d2 ♕d7 19 a5 ♕h3 20 ♖f2 ♖fe8 21 ♗f1 ♕d7 22 ♔h2 ♘b5 23 ♘xb5 axb5 with a comfortable position for Black, Zollbrecht-Miles, Biel 1995.

| 11 | ...  | 0-0  |
|----|------|------|
| 12 | a4   | a6   |
| 13 | ♗e3  | ♘fd7 |
| 14 | a5   | ♘g6  |

**15    ♖a4**

White is hoping to create pressure against the black queenside by bringing his rook to b4.

| 15 | ...  | ♘c5  |
|----|------|------|
| 16 | ♖a3  |      |

16 ♖b4 b5 17 axb6 cxb6 was an alternative. With the text White is planning the advance b4-b5 and Black must act quickly.

| 16 | ...  | ♗g5!? |
|----|------|-------|

Miles finds a very aggressive plan based on allowing his queenside to become seriously compromised in order to obtain dark-square play in the centre and on the kingside. A solid alternative was 16...♖e8 17 b4 ♘d7.

**17 ♗xc5**

After 17 f4 ♗f6 White has weakened himself along the e-file.

| 17 | ... | dxc5 |
| 18 | ♘e4 | ♗e7 |
| 19 | ♖c3 | ♖e8 |

The immediate 19...b6 is bad for Black after 20 axb6 cxb6 21 d6 White cannot now capture on c5 as 20 ♘xc5? ♗xc5 21 ♖xc5 ♕e7 hits c5 and e2. However this pawn will prove indefensible for Black in the long run and so he must turn his attention to the kingside.

**20 ♗f3**

| 20 | ... | ♗d6 |

Another way to play the position was 20...♘e5 21 ♘xc5 ♗xc5 22 ♖xc5 ♕e7 23 ♖c3 ♖ad8 when Black is a pawn down but has good control of the dark squares. However, Miles is more ambitious.

| 21 | ♘xc5 | ♕h4 |

| 22 | ♘xb7 | ♗e5 |
| 23 | ♖b3 | ♘f4 |

Although Black is two pawns down, the white forces are scattered and Black has dangerous play on the kingside. The immediate threat is ...♘xh3+. White may be able to consolidate his position with very accurate play, but the practical difficulties are immense.

**24 g3!**

An example of the difficulties facing White can be seen with the variation 24 ♖e1 ♗d4! 25 ♖xe8+ ♖xe8 26 ♕d2 ♗xf2+ 27 ♕xf2 ♖e1+ and the white queen goes. Almasi suggests that White would do better to defend with 24 ♗g4 h5 25 ♗d7 ♖e7 26 ♗c6.

| 24 | ... | ♕xh3 |

**25 d6?**

This natural move appears to be completely crushing, but Almasi has overlooked a fiendish trap. Instead 25 ♘c5 ♖ad8 leaves Black with compensation but 25 ♖e3! would have placed the onus on Black to justify his bold attacking concept, e.g. 25...♖ab8 26 ♖xe5 ♖xe5 27 gxf4 ♖e7 28 ♘c5 and White consolidates.

**25 ... ♖e6!!**
With the rook about to enter the fray on h6 Black obtains a decisive attack.

**26 dxc7**
At first sight it looks as though 26 d7 leaves Black with a hopeless position but Miles had prepared the brilliant counter 26...♖d8!.

Then after 27 ♘xd8 (if in-stead 27 ♖e1 then 27...♖h6 28 gxf4 ♖g6+ 29 ♗g4 ♖xg4+ 30 ♕xg4 ♕xg4+ 31 ♔g3 ♕xd7 32 ♘xd8 ♗xb2 leaves Black with a winning endgame) 27...♖h6 White gets mated, e.g. 28 ♖e1 ♕h2+ 29 ♔f1 ♕h1+ 30 ♗xh1 ♖xh1 is mate.

**26 ... ♗xc7**
**27 ♕d7 ♖ae8!**

**28 ♖e3**
The back rank tricks continue after 28 ♕xc7 ♕xf1+ 29 ♔xf1 ♖e1 mate.

**28 ... ♖xe3**
**29 ♕xh3 ♘xh3+**
**30 ♔g2 ♖xf3**
**0-1**
Black emerges a piece ahead.

Game 29
**Ligterink-Miles**
*Wijk aan Zee 1984*

| 1 | e4 | ♘c6 |
|---|----|-----|
| 2 | ♘f3 | d6 |
| 3 | d4 | ♘f6 |
| 4 | ♘c3 | ♗g4 |
| 5 | ♗b5 | a6 |

6    ♗xc6+    bxc6

The position is unbalanced and this promises an interesting middlegame battle. White has good control of the centre and the better pawn structure but Black has a very flexible position with the bishop pair and a useful open line on the queenside.

7    h3    ♗h5
8    ♕e2    e6

9    g4

Once White has forced the bishop to retreat, Black will find it difficult to castle quickly

on the kingside as this will be met with a quick h4-h5 and a dangerous attack. However, this advance also has its negative side. Having advanced the g-pawn, White is unlikely to want to castle on the kingside himself but Black has a ready-made attack along the b-file if the white king ends up on c1. However, quiet play promises little, e.g.

a) 9 ♗g5 ♗e7 10 0-0 0-0 11 g4 (it makes little sense to expand like this when the king is already committed to the kingside so more logical is 11 ♖ad1 ♖e8 12 ♗f4 ♕b8 13 b3 ♕b7 14 ♖fe1 d5 15 e5 ♘d7 16 ♘b1 a5 17 c3 c5 and Black has good play on the queenside, Veröci-Mohr, Belgrade 1988) 11...♗g6 12 e5 ♘d7 13 ♗f4 d5 14 ♘a4 c5 15 ♘xc5 ♘xc5 16 dxc5 ♗xc5 17 c4 f5 (Black exploits White's advances on the kingside) 18 g5 ♗h5 19 ♖fd1 c6 (White has managed to keep the kingside closed but Black has the advantage on all areas of the board) 20 ♔g2 ♗e7 21 h4 d4 22 ♖d3 c5 and Black stands well, as in Ionescu-Tomescu, Drobeta 1993.

b) 9 0-0 ♗e7 10 ♗f4 0-0 11 ♖ad1 h6 12 ♗h2 ♕b8 13 ♕e3 ♕b6 (Black avoids a trick which remains in the position for the next few moves, viz. 13...♕xb2? 14 ♖b1 and now 14...♕xc2 15 ♖fc1 traps the black queen, while 14...♕a3 is met by 15 ♘d5! and White wins

a piece) 14 ♔h1 ♗xf3 15 gxf3
♔h7 (now Black really does
threaten the b-pawn) 16 b3 d5
17 ♘a4 ♕a5 18 ♖g1 ♘d7 19
♖d3 ♗d6 with a balanced position, Neumark-Hauke, West
Germany 1988.

| 9 | ... | ♗g6 |
| 10 | ♗g5 | |

Or 10 ♘h4 d5 11 ♘xg6 hxg6
12 ♗g5 ♗e7 13 ♗xf6 ♗xf6 14
0-0-0 ♗g5+ 15 ♔b1 ♕d6 16
♘a4 ♕b4 17 b3 ♕b5 18 ♖d3
♖b8 and Black has good play,
S. Salov-Klinger, Zurich 1993.

| 10 | ... | ♗e7 |

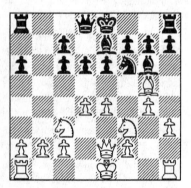

**11    0-0-0**

Others:

a) 11 ♕e3 encouraged Black
to find an unusual plan in
Matulovic-Radlovacki, Tivat
1995, e.g. 11...♘d7 (11...♕b8
would be a more normal continuation) 12 ♗xe7 ♕xe7 13
0-0-0 ♘b6 14 ♘d2 f6 (Black
hopes, at the cost of leaving
himself with a very poor pawn
structure, to contain the white
initiative by building a strong-

point on e5) 15 f4 0-0 16 ♘e2
e5 17 ♕c3 ♖ab8 18 dxe5 fxe5
19 fxe5 dxe5 20 ♖hf1 ♗f7 21
b3 g6 22 ♔b1 ♘a4 23 ♕g3
♕c5 24 ♘f3 ♖fe8 25 ♘e1 ♕a3
26 ♘d3 ♗c4 27 ♕f2 (White
goes astray in the face of
Black's continuing pressure; 27
♖d2 was the only move and left
the position unclear) 27...♖f8
28 ♕a7 ♗xd3 29 ♖xf8+ ♖xf8
30 bxa4 ♗xe2 31 ♖c1 ♕b4+ 32
♔a1 ♖b8 33 ♕xb8+ ♕xb8 34
♖b1 ♕d8 35 ♖b3 ♗c4 0-1.

b) 11 ♗xf6 ♗xf6 12 0-0-0
♕b8 13 ♕e3 ♕b6 14 h4 h5
(this demonstrates why Black
should not be too anxious to
commit his king to the kingside
in this variation) 15 g5 ♗e7 16
♘d2 d5 17 ♘b3 dxe4 18 ♘xe4
0-0 (although Black's pawn
structure is very poor it is difficult for White to keep the active
black forces under control) 19
♘ec5 ♕b5 20 ♕c3 ♖fd8 21
♖he1 a5 22 a4 ♕b4 23 ♕e3
♖ab8 24 ♘d3 ♕c4 and Black
retains a very active position,
Weiss-Sommerbauer, Austria
1993.

c) 11 e5 ♘d5 12 ♘xd5 cxd5
13 ♗xe7 ♕xe7 (White's play
has only developed Black's
pieces for him and strengthened
his centre) 14 0-0-0 c5 15 exd6
♕xd6 16 dxc5 ♕xc5 17 ♘d4
♖c8 18 h4 h5 (this move again
demonstrates why Black should
defer kingside castling for as
long as possible) 19 ♖h3 ♕c4
20 ♕d2 hxg4! 21 ♖c3 ♕xa2 22

♘b3 0-0 23 h5 ♗xh5 24 ♕g5 ♖xc3 25 bxc3 ♗g6 26 ♘d4 ♖c8 0-1 Jamieson-D. Johansen, Adelaide 1990.

**11 ... h6**

11...♘xe4!? is an interesting simplifying manoeuvre. After the forced 12 ♘xe4 ♗xe4 13 ♗xe7 ♗xf3 14 ♕xf3 ♔xe7 15 ♕xc6 Black has a good pawn structure but problems with his king, e.g. 15...♕d7 16 ♕c3 ♖hb8 17 d5 ♔f8 18 dxe6 fxe6 19 ♖he1 ♔g8 20 f4 ♖e8 21 ♖e4 ♖e7 22 b3 ♖ae8 23 ♔b2 and White gradually gained the upper hand in Groszpeter-Miles, Andorra 1995.

Also possible is 11...0-0 which leads to some forcing tactics: 12 h4 h5 13 ♗xf6 ♗xf6 14 ♘e5 ♗xh4 15 ♘xc6 ♗g5+ 16 ♔b1 ♕e8 17 gxh5 ♗h7 18 ♖hg1 ♗h6 19 d5 e5 20 ♖g2 ♔h8 21 ♖dg1 f5 22 a4 (Chandler-Keene, Melbourne 1983). If Black now trades with 22...fxe4 he has some compensation for his pawn.

**12 ♗f4**

Others:

a) 12 ♗h4?! ♘xe4! is now strong as 13 ♘xe4 can be safely met by 13...♗xh4.

b) 12 ♗xf6 ♗xf6 13 h4 h5 14 g5 ♗e7 15 ♘d2 0-0 16 ♘c4 ♕e8 (Black wants to play ...d5, but if he does so immediately, the reply 17 ♘e5, attacking c6 will be awkward) 17 f4 d5 18 ♘e5 ♗b4 19 f5 exf5 20 exf5 ♗xf5 21 ♕xh5 ♗xc3 22 bxc3 c5 (both kings are exposed but the white one proves to be easier to get at) 23 ♖hf1 ♗e4 24 ♖de1 ♕e6 25 ♖f4 cxd4 26 cxd4 ♖ab8 27 ♔d2 (White already has to run for cover) 27...♕e7 28 g6 fxg6 29 ♘xg6 ♕b4+ 30 ♔e2 ♕c4+ 31 ♔e3 ♕c3+ 32 ♔f2 ♖xf4+ 33 ♘xf4 ♕d2+ 34 ♘e2 ♖f8+ 0-1 Jordan-Miles, Melbourne 1991.

**12 ... ♕b8!**

This method of activating the queen is very typical for this variation.

**13 ♔b1 ♕b4**

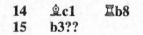

| 14 | ♗c1 | ♖b8 |
|----|-----|-----|
| 15 | b3?? | |

White thinks he has found a clever method of dealing with the threat against his knight on c3 but this is, in fact, a blunder which loses immediately.

| 15 | ... | ♕xc3! |
|----|-----|-------|
| 16 | ♗d2 | |

The black queen is trapped, but there is a simple resource.

| 16 | ... | ♘xe4 |
|----|-----|------|
| 17 | ♗e1 | |

17 ♗xc3 ♘xc3+ regains the queen and Black has an extra piece.

| 17 | ... | 0-0 |
|----|-----|-----|

**0-1**

The black queen is still trapped but White is unable to exploit this, e.g. 18 ♖d3 (or 18 h4 ♘d2+! 19 ♖xd2 ♖xb3+ 20 axb3 ♕xb3+ 21 ♔a1 ♕a3+) 18...♕c4 and the queen escapes.

### Game 30
### Kharlov-Minasian
*Moscow 1991*

| 1 | e4 | ♘c6 |
|---|----|----|
| 2 | ♘f3 | |

White can try 2 ♘c3, offering a Vienna Game after 2...e5. Black can then take up White's offer, decline with 2...e6 reaching a position discussed in chapter six (page 156), or even try 2...d6 3 d4 ♘f6 4 f4 (the only independent try) 4...e5 5 dxe5 ♗g4!? with unclear play, e.g. 6 ♕d2 dxe5 7 f5 ♗b4 8 ♕xd8+ ♖xd8 9 ♗d3 ♖d4 10 ♘ge2 ♖xe4!? Klinger-Mestrovic, Sarajevo 1988.

| 2 | ... | d6 |
|---|-----|----|
| 3 | d4 | ♘f6 |
| 4 | ♘bd2 | |

White deploys his pieces in a quiet but solid fashion. He lends support to the f3-knight (anticipating a ...♗g4 pin) and prepares to consolidate his central position with c3.

An active alternative, if White wants to avoid the standard 4 ♘c3, is 4 d5 ♘b8 5 ♘c3 g6 (5...♗g4 is another perfectly reasonable continuation) 6 ♗g5

♗g4 7 ♕d2!? (an aggressive plan from White who wants to castle quickly and launch an attack) 7...♗xf3 8 gxf3 ♘bd7 9 0-0-0 c6 10 ♔b1 ♗g7 11 ♗h6 ♗xh6 12 ♕xh6 ♕b6

13 ♗h3 (White continues very actively, ignoring the threat to his f-pawn) 13...♘e5 (better than 13...♕xf2 14 ♖hf1 ♕b6 15 f4) 14 ♖hg1 ♕xf2! (now that White has been forced to waste time with his king's rook, it is less dangerous for Black to accept this sacrifice) 15 f4 ♘c4 16 e5 ♘h5 (White has a strong initiative, but his centre is collapsing) 17 exd6 ♕xf4 18 d7+ ♔d8 19 ♖g5 ♘xb2! 20 ♔xb2 ♕b4+ 21 ♔c1 ♕xc3 22 ♖d3 ♕e1+ 23 ♔b2 ♕b4+ 24 ♖b3 ♕d4+ 25 ♔b1 f5 26 ♖xb7 ♕d1+ 27 ♔b2 ♕xd5 28 ♖xh5 c5! 29 ♕g7 ♕xb7+ 30 ♔c1 ♕h1+ 0-1 Rohde-Miles, Chicago 1990. Black has defended the a8-rook, so 31...gxh5 will win easily.

**4 ... ♗g4**

Black could transpose into a quiet line of the Pirc Defence with 4...g6, but this is more in the spirit of 1...♘c6.

**5 c3**

5 ♗b5 a6 6 ♗xc6+ bxc6 gives White the opportunity to play as in game 29, but with the option of c4, e.g. 7 0-0 e6 8 c4 ♗e7 9 ♖e1 0-0 10 h3 ♗h5 11 ♕a4 (White has created problems for Black with a direct attack against the front c-pawn, but Black can solve these with a dynamic pawn sacrifice) 11...c5 12 dxc5 ♘d7! 13 cxd6 ♗xd6

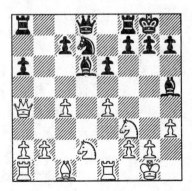

14 ♕c2 (Black's chances were clearly illustrated in the game Ostrowski-Przewoznik, Mikolajki 1991, e.g. 14 ♕d1 f5 15 exf5 exf5 16 ♕c2 ♕f6 17 ♕d3 ♖ae8 18 ♖f1 ♔h8 19 ♘b3 f4 20 ♗d2 ♘e5 21 ♘xe5 ♗xe5 22 ♗b4 ♖d8 23 ♕e4 ♖fe8 24 ♖ae1 f3 25 g3 ♗xg3 26 ♗e7 ♕xb2 27 ♕f5 ♖xe7 28 ♖b1 ♕e5 29 ♕xe5 ♗xe5 0-1) 14...f5 15 exf5 exf5 16 b3 ♘c5 17 ♘e5 ♗xe5 18 ♖xe5 ♘d3 19 ♖e3 ♕d4 20 ♖b1 ♘xf2 21 ♕c3 (Black regains his pawn; if 21 ♔xf2, then 21...f4) 21...♕xc3 22 ♖xc3 ♘d1 23 ♖d3 f4 24 ♗a3 ♖fd8 25 ♖xd8+ ♖xd8 26 ♗b4 ♗e2 27 ♘e4 f3 28 gxf3 ♗xf3 29 ♘c3 ♖d3 30 ♘xd1 ♗xd1 with a drawn endgame, Wahls-Miles, Biel 1990.

**5    ...        e6**
**6    ♗d3       d5**

As in previous examples, Black is heading for a French Defence with his bishop outside of the pawn chain.

**7    e5        ♘d7**

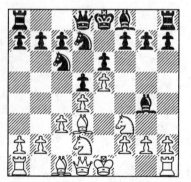

**8    h3**

8 0-0 f6 (Black does not have the thrust ...c5 immediately available, so this is the natural way to attack the centre) 9 exf6 ♕xf6 10 h3 ♗h5 11 ♕b3 0-0-0 12 ♗b5 ♘db8 13 ♕a4 ♗d6 14 b4 g5 15 ♗xc6 ♘xc6 16 b5 ♘b8 17 ♘e5 ♖hg8 (17...♗xe5 18 dxe5 ♕xe5 was about equal but Black prefers to build up his position) 18 f3 ♗e8 19 ♕xa7 ♗xb5 20 ♖b1 ♗a6 21 c4 ♗xe5 22 dxe5 ♕xe5 23 ♗b2 d4 24 ♖fe1 ♕f4 25 ♘e4 d3 and Black stands well, Yudasin-Minasian, (20-minute game) Tilburg 1993.

**8    ...        ♗h5**
**9    ♘f1       f6**
**10   ♘g3?!**

White sees that he can displace the black king by sacrificing a pawn, but his compensation turns out to be insufficient. Better was 10 g4 ♗f7 11 ♕e2 with a balanced position.

**10   ...        ♗xf3**
**11   ♕xf3      fxe5**
**12   ♕h5+**

This looks very dangerous for Black but he does in fact win a pawn in relative safety.

**12    ...    ♚e7**

Not however 12...g6? 13 ♗xg6+ hxg6 14 ♕xg6+ ♚e7 15 ♗g5+ and now 15...♚d6 might not be so bad if Black was merely losing his queen, but unfortunately 16 ♘f5 is checkmate.

**13    dxe5**

13 ♗g5+ ♘f6 14 dxe5 ♘xe5 simply transposes back to the game.

**13    ...    ♘cxe5**
**14    ♗g5+    ♘f6**
**15    0-0-0**

15 ♗e2 ♚d7 16 ♕h4 h6 17 ♗e3 was another way for White to play but the two central pawns provide an excellent barrier for the black king.

**15    ...    ♚d7!**

**16    ♕h4    h6**
**17    ♘e4!?**

17 ♗xf6 ♕xf6 and 17 ♗e3 ♘xd3+ 18 ♖xd3 ♗d6 leave White with virtually nothing for

his pawn.

**17    ...    ♗e7**
**18    ♗xf6    gxf6**

18...♘xd3+ 19 ♖xd3 gxf6 was also very good for Black.

**19    ♕h5    f5**

Black avoids the simple trap 19...dxe4?? 20 ♗b5+.

**20    ♘g3    ♕g8**

This neat move allows Black to complete his development with ...♖f8 and ...♚c8 after which White will have nothing for the pawn. White has no good way to prevent this regrouping and so the game is essentially decided.

| 21 | ♚b1 | ♖f8 |
|----|-----|-----|
| 22 | ♗c2 | ♗d6 |
| 23 | ♕e2 | f4 |
| 24 | ♕b5+ | ♚c8 |
| 25 | ♘e2 | a6 |
| 26 | ♕a4 | ♘c4 |
| 27 | ♘d4 | ♘b6 |
| 28 | ♕b3 | ♖f6 |
| 29 | ♖hg1 | e5 |
| 30 | ♘f5 | e4 |

It is bad enough being a pawn down for nothing, but facing

two huge central pawns makes White's task hopeless.

| 31 | g4 | fxg3 |
|----|-----|------|
| 32 | ♖xg3 | |

| 32 | ... | ♛f8 |

Black manages to avoid 32...♛f7? 33 ♘xd6+ ♖xd6 34 ♗xe4!, when White has chances to save the game, and the more drastic 32...♗xg3? 33 ♘e7+.

Black now won easily after 33 ♘xd6+ ♖xd6 34 ♛b4 ♛xf2 35 ♖g7 ♖hd8 36 ♛d4 ♛xd4 37 cxd4 ♘c4 38 ♖e1 ♘d2+ 39 ♔c1 ♘f3 40 ♖d1 ♖e8 41 ♖g2 ♖f6 42 ♗b3 c6 43 ♔c2 ♖f4 44 ♔c3 ♖h4 45 ♖g3 ♘g5 46 ♖h1 e3 47 ♗c2 ♖f4 48 ♖e1 ♘f3 49 ♗g6 ♘xe1 50 ♗xe8 ♘f3 51 ♔d3 ♖e4! 52 ♗g6 ♖e7 0-1.

# 4    1 d4 ♘c6 without 2 c4

|   | 1 | d4 | ♘c6 |
|---|---|----|----|

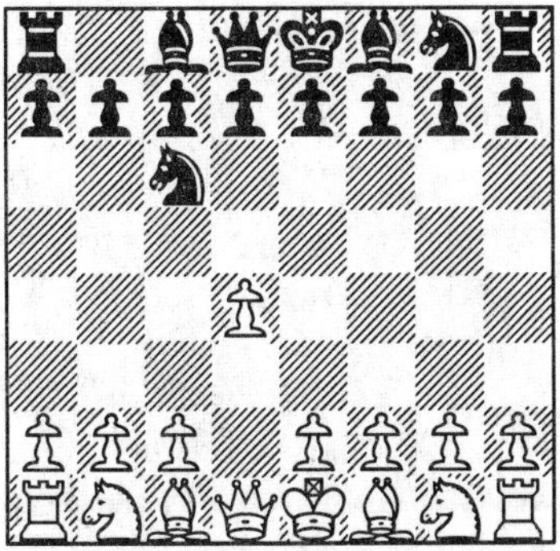

In this chapter we consider White plans which delay c4 or avoid it entirely. Broadly speaking, White can adopt three different approaches:

## 1) 2 d5 ♘e5

Here White plays what could be described as a 'mirror-image' Alekhine's Defence. He gains time and space in the centre, but must be careful not to become too carried away with thoughts of kicking the black knight around. Black remains solid and must be on the look-out for opportunities to exploit the slight dark square weaknesses which often appear in the white position.

## 2) 2 ♘f3 d5 3 c4

With this sequence White transposes directly into the Chigorin Defence (1 d4 d5 2 c4 ♘c6), but Black has sidestepped the dangerous 3 ♘c3 line and obliged White to play the less testing 3 ♘f3. White will usually obtain a strong centre and the bishop pair at the expense of a broken pawn structure and a slight lack of development. This unbalancing of the position ensures a dynamic middlegame.

## 3) 2 ♘f3 d5 3 g3

This is not a critical test of Black's opening. White develops quietly and hopes to break open the centre with c4 at a later date. However, Black can generate swift play with a combination of ...♗g4, ...♕d7 and ...0-0-0 and can look to the future with confidence.

### Game 31
### Lukacs-O'Donnell
*Budapest 1991*

| 1 | d4 | ♘c6 |
|---|----|----|
| 2 | d5 | ♘e5 |
| 3 | f4 |    |

15...♘xd2 16 ♘xd2 ♗g1.

| 3 | ... | ♘g6 |
|---|---|---|
| 4 | e4 | e6 |

4...e5 has no independent significance since White's best move is 5 dxe6. For a misguided attempt by White to avoid this simple transposition see the game Weinitschke-Bogoljubow, given in the introduction.

| 5 | dxe6 |
|---|---|

5 ♘f3 does nothing to cure White's perennial weakness in this type of position, where he is in danger of over-extension, namely a sensitivity along the g1-a7 diagonal, e.g. 5...exd5 6 exd5 ♗c5 (thematically occupying the key diagonal) 7 ♕d3 d6 8 ♘c3 ♘f6 9 ♗e2 0-0 10 ♗d2 ♘g4 11 ♘d1 ♖e8 12 h3 ♘f6 13 g4 ♘e4 14 ♖h2 ♘h4 (White now falls foul of an unusual invasion by the black pieces) 15 ♘c3 (15 ♘g5 ♘xg5 16 fxg5 ♕e7 17 ♕g3 ♗g1 and Black's neat bishop move wins material, Gerusel-Miles, Porz 1982 - see the introduction)

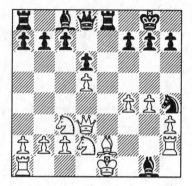

(An amazing way to win material, especially considering it has happened twice!) 17 ♖h1 ♘g2+ 18 ♔f1 ♘xf4 19 ♕f3 ♘xe2 20 ♘xe2 ♗b6 and Black went on to win, Prudnikova-Rucheva, Alushta 1992. The ...♗g1 theme is a remarkable coincidence in these two games.

| 5 | ... | fxe6 |
|---|---|---|

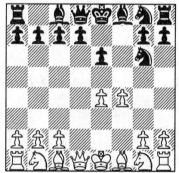

Of course, Black would not enter into this combative opening at all if he were inclined to play 5...dxe6 here. After 6 ♕xd8+ ♔xd8 7 ♘f3 Black's position is sound but quite devoid of energy.

After the recapture by the f-pawn, the pawn structure is unbalanced and Black looks for counterchances not only along the key g1-a7 diagonal, but also on the half open f-file.

**6 ♘f3**

Or:

a) 6 ♗d3 ♗c5 7 g3 d6 8 h4 (White chooses an aggressive plan but the black position is too solid to be disrupted by such early violence) 8...♗d7 9 h5 ♘f8 10 ♗d2 ♕e7 11 ♘c3 ♗c6 12 ♕e2 ♘h6 13 0-0-0 0-0-0 14 ♘f3 ♘d7 15 ♖h4 ♘f6 16 e5 ♘d5 17 exd6 cxd6 18 ♘xd5 ♗xd5 19 c4 ♗xf3 20 ♕xf3 ♘f5 21 ♖hh1 ♔b8 with a balanced position, Ballmann-Bus, Odessa 1990.

b) After 6 e5 Black could consider the immediate 6...d5, when 7 exd6 ♗xd6 leaves Black with better development and the white f-pawn rather exposed. These factors would easily compensate for the weak pawn on e6. Instead, in the game Mirallès-Maeser, Switzerland 1994, Black delayed his central counter too long, viz. 6...♗c5 7 ♘f3 ♘h6 8 ♗d3 ♘h4 9 g3 ♘xf3+ 10 ♕xf3 ♕e7 11 ♘d2 and now 11...d5 lost a pawn after 12 exd6 cxd6 13 ♗b5+ ♗d7 14 ♕xb7 ♖d8 15 ♗xd7+ ♖xd7 16 ♕a8+ and White won easily.

However best of all, and certainly consistent with the double-edged nature of the entire opening is 6...♗c5 7 ♘f3 ♘h6 8 ♗d3 0-0 9 g3 (9 ♗xg6 hxg6 10 ♘c3 b6 is unclear) 9...b6 10 ♗e4 (otherwise Black gains a smooth development with ....♗b7) 10...♗a6! and if now 11 ♗xa8 ♕xa8 Black's attacking chances more than outweigh his small material investment.

**6 ... ♗c5**
**7 ♘c3**

7 e5 transposes into 6 e5 ♗c5 7 ♘f3.

**7 ... ♘h6!**

A solid alternative is 7...d6 8 ♘a4 ♗b6 (surely it is better for Black to play 8...♗b4+ 9 c3 ♗a5 when if White wants to gain the bishop pair he is obliged to weaken his queenside with 9 b4) 9 ♘xb6 axb6 10 e5 ♘8e7 11 exd6 cxd6 12 ♗d3 0-0 13 0-0 h6 14 ♘d4 e5 15 fxe5 ♘xe5 16 ♗e2 ♖xf1+ 17 ♕xf1 ♘7c6 18 ♗e3 with a small plus for White, Ruban-Ermenkov, Miskolc 1990.

**8    ♘a4?!**

Decentralising like this does not help White's cause. Better is 8 e5 0-0! (not 8...♘g4 9 ♘e4 ♗e3 10 ♗xe3 ♘xe3 11 ♕d2 ♘xf1 12 ♖xf1 0-0 13 g3 when Black has only helped White to develop all his pieces) 9 ♘e4 (9 g3 d5 10 exd6 cxd6 11 ♘e4 ♕b6 12 c3 ½-½ Balogh-Kriz, Czech Republic 1993) 9...♗b6 10 g3 ♘f5 (a dynamic attempt by Black to exploit his lead in development is 10...d5!? 11 exd6 e5 with compensation) 11 ♕d3 d5 with an equal game.

**8    ...    ♗b4+**

A standard finesse instead of the immediate 8...♗e7, to underscore the decentralisation of White's knight. If, in response, 9 ♘c3 then, of course, 9...♗xc3+ 10 bxc3 0-0 and Black has achieved as much as he can hope for from this opening.

**9    c3    ♗e7**

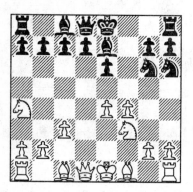

**10    c4**

White is anxious to prevent

Black from breaking in the centre (e.g. 10 g3 d5), but this move weakens his dark squares and doesn't do anything for his development. However, 10 f5!? is doubtful, e.g. 10...exf5 11 ♗xh6 gxh6 12 exf5 ♘h4 13 ♘e5 (13 ♘xh4 ♗xh4+ 14 g3 ♕e7+ is good for Black) 13...0-0 and White is insufficiently well developed to exploit Black's exposed king.

**10    ...    0-0**
**11    g3    b6**

The fianchetto development of Black's queen's bishop is a common strategic motif here.

**12    f5**

White pushes forwards, but preferable would have been a more solid course with 12 ♗h3 ♗b7 13 ♘c3 ♗c5 14 ♕e2 ♔h8 when the position is unclear.

**12    ...    ♗b4+!**

Not 12...exf5 13 ♕d5+.

**13    ♘c3**

Others are not attractive, e.g. 13 ♗d2 ♗xd2+ 14 ♕xd2 ♗b7 or 13 ♔f2 ♘g4+ 14 ♔g2 ♘6e5.

| 13 | ... | ♕f6 |
|----|-----|-----|
| 14 | ♗e2 | ♘e5 |

Black does well to avoid White's main idea, which was 14...exf5 15 ♗xh6 (15 ♕d5+ ♔h8 16 ♕xa8 ♗xc3+ 17 bxc3 ♕xc3+ 18 ♔d1 ♕xa1 19 exf5 ♘xf5 20 ♕xa7 ♘e3+ 21 ♔d2 ♘e5 is terrible for White) 15...♗xc3+ 16 bxc3 fxe4 17 0-0 ♕d6 (not 17...gxh6 18 ♕d5+ ♕e6 19 ♕xa8 exf3 20 ♗xf3) 18 ♕xd6 cxd6 19 ♗c1! exf3 20 ♗xf3 ♖b8 21 ♗d5+ ♔h8 22 ♖xf8+ ♘xf8 23 ♗a3 when Black is completely hamstrung in the endgame.

| 15 | 0-0 |
|----|-----|

| 15 | ... | ♗xc3 |
|----|-----|------|

After 15...♗b7 16 ♗xh6 gxh6 17 ♘xe5 ♕xe5 18 ♕xd7 ♗xc3 19 bxc3 exf5 20 ♖xf5 ♕xe4 21 ♖xf8+ ♖xf8 22 ♕g4+ ♕xg4 23 ♗xg4 Black has a tiny edge in the endgame. The text leads to complications which are soon followed by mass simplification.

| 16 | bxc3 | ♗b7 |
|----|------|-----|

| 17 | ♘xe5 | ♕xe5 |
|----|------|------|
| 18 | ♕xd7 | ♘xf5 |
| 19 | exf5 | ♕xe2 |
| 20 | ♕xe6+ | ♕xe6 |
| 21 | fxe6 | ♖xf1+ |
| 22 | ♔xf1 | ♗a6 |

Black will now win a pawn but it is not enough to win the game.

| 23 | ♗f4 | ♗xc4+ |
|----|-----|-------|
| 24 | ♔f2 | ♖e8 |
| 25 | ♗xc7 | ♖xe6 |
| 26 | ♖e1 | ♖xe1 |
| 27 | ♔xe1 | ♗xa2 |
| 28 | ♗b8 | a6 |
| 29 | ♗c7 | b5 |
| 30 | ♔d2 | ♔f7 |
| 31 | ♔c1 | ♗e6 |
| 32 | h4 | ♔e7 |
| 33 | ♔b2 | ♔d7 |
| 34 | ♗e5 | ½-½ |

### Game 32
### Shestoperov-Bus
*Krasnodar 1991*

| 1 | d4 | ♘c6 |
|---|-----|-----|
| 2 | d5 | ♘e5 |
| 3 | e4 | e6 |

**4    ♘f3**

If White is reluctant to commit himself to 4 f4, then other options are:

a) 4 ♕d4 ♘g6 5 ♘c3 b6 6 ♘f3 ♗b7 7 h4 e5 8 ♕c4 (not 8 ♘xe5 ♗c5) 8...h5 9 ♗g5 ♘f6 10 g3 a6 11 ♗h3 ♗d6 12 ♘d1 c5 13 ♘e3 b5 14 ♕e2 ♕a5+ 15 c3 ♗f8 16 ♘d2 d6 17 ♕f3 ♘g8 Messarius-Remmeke, Germany 1992. Following some exotic manoeuvring on both sides a fairly normal, and more or less equal, position has arisen. For further analysis of 4 ♕d4, see the game Tisdall-Jacobs in the introduction.

b) 4 c4 is dubious as it weakens the dark squares. Di Stefano-Rossi, Zurich 1988 provided a good example of why this is not a good idea: 4...♗c5 5 ♘f3? ♘g4 6 ♘d4 ♘xf2! 7 ♔xf2 ♕f6+ 8 ♔e3 e5 and White is already hopelessly lost.

**4    ...    ♘xf3+**

4...♕f6 is also possible, e.g. 5 ♗e2 ♘xf3+ (5...♗c5 6 ♘c3 a6

7 0-0 ♘g4 8 h3 h5 is far less convincing for Black, Sämisch-Nimzowitsch, Baden-Baden 1925) 6 ♗xf3 e5 7 ♗e3 ♗b4+ 8 c3 ♗e7 9 ♕d2 ♕g6 10 c4 ♘f6 11 ♘c3 0-0 12 ♕e2 ♗b4 13 ♗d2 d6 14 h3 ♘e8 15 g4 ♕f6 16 h4 ♕e7 17 0-0-0 c5 18 ♖dg1 a6 19 g5 b5 with counterplay as in Fishdick-Przewoznik, Dortmund 1992.

**5    ♕xf3    ♕f6**
**6    ♗e2**

Trading queens with 6 ♕xf6 ♘xf6 7 dxe6 fxe6 8 ♗d3 gives Black wonderfully free development after 8...♗c5 followed by ...e5 and ...d6

| 6 | ... | ♗c5 |
|---|---|---|
| 7 | ♘c3 | ♕xf3 |
| 8 | ♗xf3 | e5 |
| 9 | 0-0 | a6 |
| 10 | ♗d2 | d6 |
| 11 | a4 | |

Black has obviously emerged from the opening with no problems. The only question is when to time his freeing thrust with ...f5.

**11 ... f5**

Black can also consider preparing this thrust with ...♘e7 and ...0-0.

**12 exf5 ♗xf5**
**13 ♘e4 ♗xe4**

This gives White the bishop pair and leaves Black with a rather inflexible position. A better continuation is 13...♗a7, intending ...♘f6 and Black has equal chances.

**14 ♗xe4 ♘f6**
**15 ♗f3 0-0**
**16 b4 ♗a7**
**17 c4 ♗d4**

In spite of White's bishops and mobile queenside pawns, the activity of Black's one remaining bishop still gives him sufficient counterplay to hold the balance.

**18 ♖a3 b6**
**19 a5 ♖fb8**
**20 g4**

In this position, there is little more that White can achieve on the queen's flank, given that Black's bishop controls a1. He therefore tries to gain space on the other wing.

**20 ... h6**
**21 h4 e4**

Just in time. This comes at a moment when White's bishop cannot retreat and still maintain its attack on e4.

**22 ♗e2**

If 22 ♗g2, then 22...♘xg4 23 ♗xe4 ♖f8, when Black has nothing to fear.

**22 ... ♘d7**

**23 ♖d1 bxa5**
**24 ♖xa5 ♖f8**
**25 ♗e3 ♗c3**
**26 ♖b1 ♖fb8**
**27 ♖a4**

If White now had time to consolidate with ♖b3 then he might be getting somewhere, but the general activity of Black's pieces suggests that he will always have a saving clause. This now arrives in the form of a tactical trick to force a drawn endgame.

**27 ... ♘c5**
**28 ♗xc5 dxc5**

| 29 | b5 | axb5 |
|----|-----|------|
| 30 | ♖xa8 | ♖xa8 |
| 31 | ♖xb5 | ♗d4 |
| 32 | ♔g2 | ♖a2 |
| 33 | ♔f1 | ♔f7 |
| 34 | ♖b7 | ♗e5 |
| 35 | ♖b5 | ♗d6 |
| 36 | ♖b3 | ♗f4 |
| 37 | ♖b5 | ♗d6 |
| 38 | ♖b3 | ♗f4 |
| 39 | ♖b5 | ½-½ |

**Transposition to Chigorin's Defence**

Game 33
**Piza-Novak**
*Bratislava 1991*

| 1 | d4 | ♘c6 |
|---|-----|------|
| 2 | ♘f3 | d5 |
| 3 | c4 | ♗g4 |

| 4 | cxd5 | ♗xf3 |
|---|------|------|
| 5 | gxf3 | |

For White's other main continuation, 5 dxc6, see the next game.

| 5 | ... | ♕xd5 |
|---|-----|------|
| 6 | e3 | e6 |

For many years the automatic move in this position was 6...e5 but then there came the gradual realisation that opening the position really did help to reinforce White's advantage of the bishop pair. The modern move is the more restrained 6...e6, which actually does achieve Black's ambition of hampering the free play of the white bishops.

| 7 | ♘c3 | |

| 7 | ... | ♕h5 |

Black often plays 7...♗b4 here, but this queen move, which eyes up the broken white kingside, has more to recommend it. Therefore we select this as our main variation.

| 8 | ♗e2 | |

Experience indicates that offering a speedy trade of queens does not promise White anything. The text looks more logical in that White prepares to harass the black queen and swiftly realign his king's bishop along the powerful h1-a8 diagonal.

Here is a brief summary of the alternatives:

a) 8 ♗d2 0-0-0 9 f4 ♕xd1+ 10 ♖xd1 ♘f6 11 ♗g2 ♘e7 12 ♖c1 ♔b8 13 ♔e2 ♘f5 14 ♖hd1 h6 15 ♔f1 ♗e7 16 ♘e2 g5 17 ♗a5 ♖d7 18 ♗h1 ♘d6 19 ♖c2 c6 20 ♖cc1 ♘d5 21 ♗g2 f5 with an equal endgame, Dumitrache-Atalik, Bucharest 1995.

b) 8 f4 ♕xd1+ 9 ♔xd1 ♘f6 (9...0-0-0 10 ♗d2 ♘f6 11 ♗b5 ♘e7 12 ♔e2 ♘f5 13 ♖ac1 ♗e7 14 ♗d3 ♔b8 15 ♖hg1 g6 16 ♘a4 h6 17 ♘c5 ♖hg8 18 ♘b3 g5 19 fxg5 hxg5 with a balanced position, Karpov-Miles, Bugojno 1986) 10 ♗g2 0-0-0 11 ♔e2 ♘e7

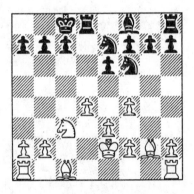

12 ♘e4 (12 ♗d2 h6 13 ♘b5 ♔b8 14 ♘a3 g5 15 fxg5 hxg5 16 ♖ag1 ♘f5 17 ♘c4 ♗e7 18 ♗f3 ♘d5 19 ♘e5 ♖h7 20 ♗e4 f6 21 ♘f3 ♖h6 22 ♗c2 ♘h4 23 a3 ♗d6 and the weak h-pawn is a permanent headache for White, Bareev-Kamsky, Tilburg 1991) 12...♘xe4 13 ♗xe4 h6 14

♗d2 g5 15 fxg5 hxg5 16 ♖ag1 f5 17 ♗c2 ♖h5 18 ♗b3 ♔d7 19 f3 ♗g7 20 ♖g2 ♖dh8 21 ♔d3 ♗f6 22 e4 fxe4+ 23 fxe4 ♖h3+ 24 ♗e3 ♘g6 25 ♔d2 ♘h4 26 ♖f2 ♘f3+ 27 ♔d3 g4 28 ♗d1 ♗h4 29 ♖ff1 ♘xh2 30 ♗xg4 ♖xe3+ 31 ♔xe3 ♘xg4+ 32 ♔d3 e5 and Black went on to win, Brunner-Short, Solingen 1986.

| **8** | **...** | **♘ge7** |

The knight is developed here rather than on f6 in order to provide back-up for the black knight on c6. Black wants to castle queenside without having his entire pawn-front shattered by an inopportune ♗xc6.

| **9** | **f4** | **♕h4** |
| **10** | **♗f3** | **0-0-0** |
| **11** | **♗d2** | |

| **11** | **...** | **♔b8?** |

Black fails to appreciate the knife-edged nature of this situation and plays a safety move which in fact amounts to a loss of a vital tempo. The correct way to proceed here is with immense and immediate force, thus 11...g5 12 fxg5 h6 13 gxh6 ♗xh6 when Black's lead in development and ability to operate with tactical threats involving ...♘xd4, ...♖hg8 and ...e5 give him plenty of compensation for the pawn.

A more testing line is 12 fxg5 h6 13 ♘e4 hxg5 14 ♖c1 when Black's best is 14...e5, starting an immediate tactical firefight in the centre.

**12     ♖c1**

White is now threatening to win quite effortlessly by concentrating his forces directly against the black king with moves such as ♘e4-c5 and ♕b3. Black cannot stand idly by and watch his own slaughter. He must generate instant counterplay.

**12     ...     g5**
**13     fxg5**

For his part White cannot ignore Black's demonstration. After 13 ♘e4 gxf4 14 ♘c5 fxe3 15 ♗xe3 ♘xd4 White's attack should not be sound.

**13     ...     ♖g8**
**14     ♘e4     ♘d5** (D)
**15     a3?**

With the board in flames White now conceives an attacking strategy that is inappropriately elephantine. White should take his life in his hands with the exchange sacrifice 15 ♖xc6 bxc6 16 ♕a4, following with ♔e2 and ♖c1 when Black is in extreme jeopardy.

**15     ...     h6**
**16     b4**

16 ♖xc6 is still possible.

**16     ...     hxg5**
**17     b5     ♘ce7**
**18     ♘c5     ♘c8**

White has gone to immense lengths to establish his knight on c5, but now Black has managed to arrange plenty of defenders around his goal-mouth and his own counterattack is due to start.

**19     a4     g4**
**20     ♗g2**

**20     ...     ♖g5**

Preparing an exchange sacrifice which gains control of the dark squares and leaves White's king displaced.

| 21 | e4 | ♗xc5 |
|----|----|----|

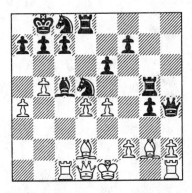

| 22 | ♗xg5 |
|----|----|

It is more than likely that White had been relying here on playing 22 ♖xc5 when Black appears to lose a mass of material but then he has the cunning riposte 22...♘e3!! 23 ♗xe3 ♖xc5 when the pin on the d-file means that it is White who loses material.

| 22 | ... | ♗b4+ |
|----|----|----|
| 23 | ♔f1 | ♕xg5 |
| 24 | exd5 | exd5 |

For all practical purposes the game is decided. White's position is so completely disorganised that it is merely a matter of time before Black's forces gather for the decisive punch. Having missed his own chance to sacrifice the exchange White has to watch helplessly as Black's counter sacrifice gathers momentum.

| 25 | h4 | ♕f4 |
|----|----|----|
| 26 | ♖c2 | ♘d6 |
| 27 | h5 | ♘f5 |
| 28 | h6 | |

Instead of struggling on with 28 ♔g1 which could be met by 28...♘xd4 29 ♖b2 ♗c5 for example, White tries the hopelessly optimistic text.

| 28 | ... | ♘e3+ |
|----|----|----|
| 29 | ♔e2 | ♘xd1 |
| 30 | h7 | ♕xf2+ |
| 31 | ♔xd1 | ♕xd4+ |
| 32 | ♔c1 | 0-1 |

### Game 34
### Granda-Morozevich
*Amsterdam 1995*

| 1 | d4 | d5 |
|---|----|----|
| 2 | c4 | ♘c6 |
| 3 | ♘f3 | ♗g4 |
| 4 | cxd5 | ♗xf3 |
| 5 | dxc6 | |

This is one of the oldest lines in this opening and was frequently employed against Chigorin. White foregoes the advantage of the bishop pair, but hopes to avoid any damage to his pawn structure and also speculates on being able to gain time by advancing the central pawns to attack Black's queen's bishop. On the whole, though, Black's free piece play has generated very good Black results in this line.

| 5 | ... | ♗xc6 |
|---|-----|------|
| 6 | ♘c3 | e6 |

As we have already noted in the introduction an interesting alternative is the gambit 6...♘f6 7 f3 (planning e4) 7...e5 8 dxe5 ♕xd1+ and whether White recaptures with king or knight Black proceeds with the plan of ...♘d7, ...0-0-0, ...♗c5, and, if necessary, ...♖he8 and ...f6. when White's tardy development and straggling pawns give Black plenty of compensation.

| 7 | e4 |
|---|-----|

Others:

a) 7 e3 is much too passive to create problems for Black, e.g. 7...♘f6 8 f3 ♗d6 9 ♗b5 ♗xb5 10 ♘xb5 ♗b4+ 11 ♗d2 ♗xd2+

12 ♕xd2 0-0 13 0-0 a6 with a completely equal position, Gonzalez-I. Ivanov, Manresa 1993.

b) 7 ♗f4 has also not served White particularly well. This bishop is probably needed to defend either c3 or d4. For example: 7...♘f6 8 e3 ♗b4 9 ♕b3 ♘d5 10 ♗g3 0-0 11 ♗d3 ♕g5, was Teichmann-Chigorin, Cambridge Springs 1904. For full notes to this game, see the introduction.

Alternatively, 7...♘e7 8 e3 ♘g6 9 ♗g3 a6 10 ♕b3 ♗e7 11 0-0-0 0-0 12 d5 exd5 13 ♘xd5 ♕c8 and Black had no cause for complaint, Teichmann-Chigorin, Berlin 1897.

| 7 | ... | ♗b4 |
|---|-----|------|
| 8 | f3 | |

| 8 | ... | ♕h4+ |
|---|-----|------|

Another try here for Black is 8...f5!? as played in the game Pillsbury-Chigorin, St Petersburg 1896. However the pawn sacrifice 9 ♗c4 fxe4 10 0-0, as recommended by Pollock in 1896, is highly risky for Black.

See the introduction for further analysis of this game.

Black's queen check here is typical of situations where White has played f3. The idea is to loosen White's entire central and kingside pawn structure and to reposition Black's queen on h5 where it can target the soft spot on f3.

**9      g3**

**9      ...        ♕h5**

Nevertheless, also possible is 9...♕f6 10 ♗e3 0-0-0 e.g. 11 ♗g2 (11 ♗d3 ♗a5 12 0-0 ♗b6 13 e5 ♕e7 14 ♗e4 with an unclear position) 11...♗c5 12 e5 ♕e7 13 0-0 f6 (Black has strong pressure against the white centre) 14 f4 ♗xg2 15 ♔xg2 ♗b6 16 ♖f2 ♘h6 17 ♖d2 ♘f5 18 ♗f2 h5 19 ♖c1 ♔b8 20 ♘a4 ♖d5 and Black's firm control over the central light squares gives him excellent chances, Moiseenko-Kobaliya, St Petersburg 1995.

**10      ♗e2**

10 ♗g2 0-0-0 11 a3 ♗c5 12

♘e2 ♗b6 13 ♘f4 ♕a5+ 14 ♗d2 ♕b5 15 ♗c3 ♘f6 16 a4 ♕g5 17 e5 ♘d5 18 ♘xd5 ♗xd5 (as with the previous example, Black has encouraged White to advance in the centre and can now hope to exploit the weaknesses thus created) 19 ♗d2 ♕g6 20 ♗e3 a6 21 a5 ♗a7 22 0-0 h5 23 ♖c1 ♖d7 24 ♖f2 h4 Houshan-Wittmann, Lucerne Ol 1982. The white kingside is weak and the pawn on d4 is a target. Black has all the chances.

**10      ...        0-0-0**

Setting the evil trap 11 0-0? ♖xd4 12 ♕xd4 ♗c5 winning White's queen.

**11      ♗e3        f5**

Although this implies the sacrifice of a pawn this thematic thrust against White's central installations is much better times here than on move eight, where Chigorin originally tried it.

**12      ♕b3        ♗xc3+**
**13      bxc3        fxe4**

14 **♕xe6+** **♗d7**
15 **♕xe4**

15 ... **♖e8?!**

Black can gain more effective counterplay with 15...♘f6 16 ♕e5 ♕f7 with ...♖he8 to come.

16 **♕d3**

Now White's queen is out of the firing line on the e-file.

16 ... **♘e7**
17 **c4** **♘f5**

Black's knight eyes the weak e3-square.

18 **♗f4** **♗a4**
19 **♔f2**

Black still has good counterplay as the white king will never be able to find a safe haven.

19 ... **♖hf8**
20 **h4** **♕g6**
21 **♖ab1** **♕f6**

Black hopes for 22 ♗e5 ♖xe5 23 dxe5 ♕xe5 threatening both ...♕xg3+ and ...♕xc5+. However, White can defend well against the immediate threats to d4 by means of the following subtle retreat.

22 **♗d1** **♗d7**
23 **d5** **♕e7**
24 **♖b3** **♕c5+**
25 **♔g2** **♖f7**
26 **♕d2** **♖fe7**

His control of the e-file and the weak dark squares in White's camp still give Black good compensation for his pawn. Note that Black avoids 26...♕xc4? 27 ♖c3.

27 **♗g5** **♖e5**
28 **♗f4** **♘e3+**

Black gets carried away with his initiative. The logical conclusion to the game was

♕xc4 ♕d5 14 ♕d3 ♗f5 15 ♕d2 ♘g6 16 ♖ac1 ♖fd8 17 ♕e1 ♗e4 with a firm hold on the central light squares, Ye Rongguang-Manor, Thessaloniki Ol 1988.

| 6 | ... | ♗xc3+ |
|---|---|---|
| 7 | bxc3 | |

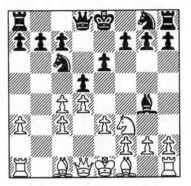

| 7 | ... | ♘ge7 |
|---|---|---|

7...♘f6 8 cxd5 exd5 9 h3 ♗h5 10 c4 0-0 11 ♗b2 ♘e4 12 ♕a4 a6 13 ♕c2 ♗g6 14 ♗d3 ♖e8 15 0-0 is playable for Black, Spraggett-Perovic, Vienna 1990. Black has a normal queenside position with his bishop outside the pawn chain.

| 8 | cxd5 | exd5 |
|---|---|---|
| 9 | c4 | |

With Black's queen's bishop so active, the two bishops are not such a huge plus in this situation, so White tries to make the most of his slight central pawn majority. 9 ♖b1 should be met by 9...♖b8 while 9 a4 0-0 10 ♗a3 ♖e8 11 ♗b5 ♘g6 12 ♗xc6 bxc6 13 h3 ♗f5 with sufficient control over the light

squares to compensate for the weakened black queenside.

| 9 | ... | 0-0 |
|---|---|---|
| 10 | ♗d3 | ♘g6 |
| 11 | h3 | |

| 11 | ... | ♗xf3 |
|---|---|---|
| 12 | gxf3 | |

White avoids the natural 12 ♕xf3 on account of 12...dxc4 13 ♗xc4 ♘xd4 14 exd4 ♕xd4 forking a1 and c4.

| 12 | ... | dxc4 |
|---|---|---|
| 13 | ♗xc4 | ♕f6 |

Black has everything he wants from the opening. Although White, as so often, has a big pawn centre and two bishops against two knights, Black's development is far superior and he can start to pound White both on the central files and on the kingside where White's pawns are shattered.

| 14 | ♔f1 | ♘ce7 |
|---|---|---|
| 15 | ♗b2 | ♖ad8 |
| 16 | ♗d3 | ♘h4 |
| 17 | f4 | c5 |
| 18 | ♖c1 | cxd4 |
| 19 | ♗xd4 | |

Just as White's bishops appear to be co-ordinating Black eliminates White's hopes by sacrificing the exchange. In subsequent play Black's agile knights prove superior.

| 19 | ... | ♖xd4 |
|----|-----|------|
| 20 | exd4 | ♕xf4 |
| 21 | ♖c4 | ♘f3 |
| 22 | ♔g2 | ♘g6 |

**23   ♗xg6**

Not 23 ♕xf3 ♘h4+, but the text only increases Black's power on the f-file.

| 23 | ... | fxg6 |
|----|-----|------|
| 24 | ♕e2 | ♕g5+ |

| 25 | ♔f1 | ♘d2+ |
|----|-----|------|
| 26 | ♔e1 | ♘xc4 |
| 27 | ♕xc4+ | ♔h8 |
| 28 | ♔f1 | ♕f4 |

A pawn down and with a shattered position further resistance is futile.

| 29 | ♕e2 | ♕xd4 |
|----|-----|------|
| 30 | ♔g2 | ♕d5+ |
| 31 | f3 | ♕g5+ |
| 32 | ♔h2 | ♕f4+ |
| 33 | ♔g2 | h5 |
| 34 | ♖d1 | ♖f5 |
| 35 | ♕f2 | ♖g5+ |
| 36 | ♔h1 | |

| 36 | ... | ♖g3 |
|----|-----|------|

| 37 | ♖d4 | ♖xh3+ |
|----|-----|--------|
| 38 | ♔g2 | ♕h2+ |
|    | **0-1** | |

## Game 36
**Radulov-Lorenz**
*Bad Mergentheim 1989*

| 1 | d4 | ♘c6 |
|---|-----|-----|
| 2 | ♘f3 | d5 |
| 3 | g3 | |

Of White's third move alternatives which side-step the main lines, the kingside fianchetto is the most testing. 3 ♗g5 would actively assist Black, since he can strike out at the white bishop with ...f6 at some moment. 3 ♗f4 ♗g4 4 e3 e6 5 ♗b5 ♗d6 followed by ...♘ge7 is not dangerous.

A curiosity was the strange encounter Langeweg-Dückstein, Zurich 1975 which finished abruptly after 3 ♗f4 ♗g4 4 e3 e6 5 c4 ♗b4+ 6 ♘bd2 ♘f6 7 cxd5 ♘e4 and here White resigned!

However subsequent analysis

demonstrated that 8 dxc6 ♘xd2 9 ♔e2 ♕d5 10 ♕a4 ♗xf3+ 11 gxf3 ♕xf3+ 12 ♔d3 ♕e4+ 13 ♔e2 would be a draw by perpetual check. In this line though, Graham Burgess has pointed out that Black can try 9...b5!! and if 10 a3 (10 ♕c2 is stronger but Black is still well on top) 10...♕d5 11 axb4 ♘xf3.

A much better reply to 5...♗b4+ is 6 ♘c3 when a possible line is 6...♘ge7 7 ♖c1 (7 h3 ♗h5 8 ♖c1 0-0 9 a3 ♗xc3+ 10 ♖xc3 dxc4 11 ♖xc4 ♘g6 12 ♗h2 ♗xf3 13 ♕xf3 e5, Akesson-Morozevich, Lloyds Bank, London 1994 was also fine for Black) 7...0-0 8 ♗d3 ♘g6 9 h3 ♗h5 10 ♗h2 ♘h4 11 g4 ♘xf3+ 12 ♕xf3 ♗g6 13 ♗xg6 hxg6 14 cxd5 exd5 15 ♔f1 ♘e7 and Black stands well, van Wely-Morozevich, Tilburg 1993.

| 3 | ... | ♗g4 |
|---|-----|-----|
| 4 | ♗g2 | ♕d7 |

This gives the variation its distinctive flavour. Black plans to castle queenside, possibly trade off White's king's bishop with ...♗h3 and where necessary he will resort to ...f6 to fence White out of the central zone.

**5    0-0**

Others:

a) 5 h3 ♗f5

6 c4 (6 ♘e5 ♘xe5 7 dxe5 0-0-0 8 c3 f6 9 ♗f4 e6 10 ♘d2 fxe5 11 ♗xe5 ♘e7 12 ♗f4 ♘c6 13 ♘f3 ♗e4 14 0-0 ♗d6 15 ♗xd6 ♕xd6 16 ♘d4 ♗xg2 17 ♔xg2 ♘e7 18 e3 c5 19 ♘c2 ♔b8 and Black's excellent central control guarantees him the advantage, Kaenel-Landenbergue, Switzerland 1993) 6...dxc4 7 ♕a4 e5 8 dxe5 ♘xe5 9 ♕xd7+ ♘xd7 10 ♘c3 (after this White never regains his pawn so 10 ♘bd2 looks better, but after 10...0-0-0 Black has nothing to complain of) 10...c6 11 ♗e3 ♗b4 12 ♖c1 ♘gf6 13 0-0 ♘b6 14 ♗d4 0-0 15 ♗xf6 gxf6 16 ♘d4 ♗e6 17 ♘e4 f5 18 ♘f6+ ♔h8 with a good extra pawn as in the game Landen-

bergue-Hölzl, Bern 1990.

It is interesting that Landenbergue, although a noted ...♘c6 system specialist, was unable to demonstrate a convincing line when himself confronted with the opening.

b) 5 c4 e6 6 0-0 0-0-0 7 ♘c3 dxc4 (once the white queen's knight is committed to c3 it makes good sense for Black to make this capture) 8 ♕a4 ♔b8 (not 8...♗b4, which led to a swift disaster in Kumaran-Miles, Dublin Zonal 1993: 9 ♘e5 ♘xe5 10 ♕xa7 c6 11 ♗f4 ♗d6 12 ♕a8+ ♔c7 13 ♘b5+ ♔b6 14 ♕a7+ ♔xb5 15 a4+

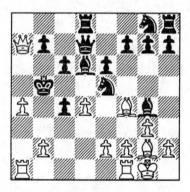

1-0) 9 ♖d1 ♗xf3 10 ♗xf3 ♘b4 11 ♕a5 ♘f6 12 a3 ♘bd5 13 e4 b6 14 ♕a6 ♘xc3 15 bxc3 ♕c6 16 a4 (White's centre is dropping off so he must launch a quick attack) 16...♘xe4 17 a5 f5 18 axb6 axb6 19 ♗f4 ♕b7 (better is 19...♗d6 20 ♗xd6 cxd6) 20 ♕xc4 ♗d6 21 ♕xe6 ♖de8 22 ♕d7 (White missed a good chance here with 22 ♕xf5 the idea being to meet the capture 22...♗xf4 with 23 ♖e1! and White stands well) 22...♗xf4 23 gxf4 ♖hf8 with an unclear position, Loginov-Wells, Harkany 1994.

c) 5 ♘e5 ♘xe5 6 dxe5 e6 7 c4 c6 (Black has a solid position although there is no reason for White to go into self-destruct as in this game) 8 ♕d4 f5 9 ♘c3 c5 10 ♕d1 d4 11 ♘b5 a6 12 ♕a4 ♖b8 13 ♘d6+ ♗xd6 14 ♕xd7+ ♔xd7 15 exd6 ♔xd6 with a winning position for Black, Karlsson-Hector, Oslo 1994.

d) 5 c3 ♗h3 6 0-0 ♗xg2 7 ♔xg2 0-0-0 8 b4 f6 9 ♘bd2 e5 10 b5 e4 11 bxc6 exf3+ 12 ♘xf3 ♕xc6 13 ♕b3 ♘e7 14 a4 ♘f5 15 a5 g5 (this is an important prelude to Black's kingside attack, as if 15...h5, 16 h4) 16 a6 b6 17 ♘e1 h5 18 ♘d3 ♕e6 19 ♖e1 h4 (Black suddenly has a very powerful attack) 20 e4 hxg3 21 fxg3

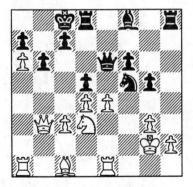

21...♘xg3 22 ♘f2 ♘f5 23

♗xg5 ♕g8 24 exf5 ♕xg5+ 0-1 Mellado-Pascual, Barbera del Valles 1995. This game is a fine advertisement for Black's system.

| 5 | ... | 0-0-0 |

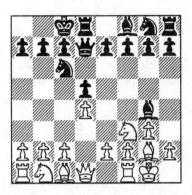

| 6 | c3 |

White's problem is that 6 c4 can be met in standard fashion, as we have seen, by 6...dxc4, so White is somewhat short of active alternatives. The text plans a queenside pawn storm with b4 against the black king. Other ideas are:

a) 6 ♖e1 f6 7 c4 (White's 6th and 7th moves do not really go together) 7...dxc4 8 ♘c3 e5 9 d5 ♘b4 10 ♗e3 ♘e7 11 d6 ♘f5 12 ♗xa7 ♕xd6 13 ♕a4 ♕c6 14 ♖ed1 ♕xa4 15 ♖xd8+ ♔xd8 16 ♘xa4 ♘c6 and White did not have much compensation for his pawn, Miles-Geenen, Moscow Ol 1994.

b) 6 ♗f4 f6 7 c4 e6 8 cxd5 exd5 9 ♘c3 g5 10 ♗d2 ♗h3 11 ♕a4 h5 12 e4 (classic chess theory says that a wing attack is best met by central counterplay, but this thrust leaves White horribly weak on the h1-a8 diagonal) 12...dxe4 13 ♘xe4 g4 14 ♘h4 ♕d5 and White is in big trouble, Frois-Fioramonti, Haifa 1989.

c) 6 ♘bd2 f6 7 b4 e5 8 dxe5 ♗xb4 9 exf6 ♘xf6 10 ♖b1 ♖he8 11 c3 ♗c5 12 ♘b3 ♗b6 13 ♘bd4 h6 14 ♗f4 g5 15 ♘xc6 ♕xc6 16 ♘e5 ♕e6 17 ♘xg4 ♘xg4 18 ♗c1

18...♗xf2+ 19 ♖xf2 ♘xf2 20 ♕b3 (20 ♔xf2 ♕f5+) 20...♕a6 21 ♗xd5 ♖xd5 22 ♕xd5 ♘e4 23 ♖b3 ♘d6 24 ♖b2 ♖xe2 25 ♖xe2 ♕xe2 and Black won easily, Weindl-Arkhipov, Kecskemet 1992. Another classic Black win in this line.

**6 ... f6**

This is a key move for Black in this variation. It creates the options of a central break with ...e5 and kingside play with ...g5. The latter move can also prove useful for dislodging an annoying white bishop from f4.

**7 b4 h5**

Off though it may look 7...g5 is probably more accurate since White should now have played 8 h4 to slow down Black's kingside advance.

**8 ♘bd2 g5**

If White tries to block the black onslaught with h4 in the future Black has ...♗xf3 followed by ...gxh4 splintering White's defences.

**9 ♘b3 e6**
**10 ♖b1 ♕h7**

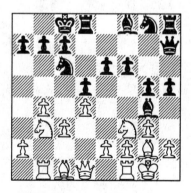

The upshot of the opening is that Black already has an enor-

mous lead in the race to attack
the opposing king. The black
queen is already on a powerful
diagonal (threatening ...♕xb1)
and has moved by express to an
extremely threatening position
on the h-file. If White invades
with ♘c5 at a later date Black
can, in principle, remove it with
...♗xc5 if the knight becomes
too threatening.

| 11 | ♗e3 | h4 |
|----|-----|-----|
| 12 | gxh4 | ♗f5 |
| 13 | hxg5 | ♗d6 |

White relies on giving up the
exchange on b1 to abate the
black attack, but Black refuses
to be deflected from his goal.

| 18 | ... | ♖xg5 |
|----|-----|-----|
| 19 | ♕xg5 | |

If 19 hxg5 then 19...♗h2+ 20
♔h1 ♗f4+ is good enough.

| 19 | ... | ♖g8 |
|----|-----|-----|
| 20 | ♕e3 | |

If 20 ♕d2 then 20...♘g6 21
e3 ♗e4.

| 20 | ... | ♘g6 |
|----|-----|-----|
| 21 | c4 | ♗e4 |
| 22 | ♕c3 | ♘xh4 |

| 14 | h4 | fxg5 |
|----|-----|-----|
| 15 | ♗xg5 | ♘ge7 |
| 16 | b5 | ♘b8 |
| 17 | ♖c1 | ♖dg8 |
| 18 | ♕d2 | |

White is struggling both to
open a line on the queenside
against Black's king and to
stem Black's tide on the other
flank. The text, however, walks
into a fresh sacrifice.

| 23 | ♖fd1 | |
|----|-----|-----|

If 23 ♘xh4 ♕xh4 24 f3, then
24...♖xg2+ forces mate.

| 23 | ... | ♘xg2 |
|----|-----|-----|

**0-1**

# 5  1 d4 ♘c6 2 c4 e5

| 1 | d4 | ♘c6 |
|---|-----|------|
| 2 | c4 | e5 |

In this chapter we consider the variations where White declines to play the obscure positions resulting from the critical 2 d5 and instead aims to steer the game into calmer, and perhaps more familiar, waters. In our opinion this is less testing for Black than the direct 2 d5, but these variations nevertheless require close study.

After 3 d5 ♘ce7, Black could, if so inclined, probably work his way into the main lines of the King's Indian Defence or Modern by continuing with ...d6 and ...g6. However, transposing back into main lines is not consistent with the phi-

losophy behind playing 1...♘c6 and so here we consider alternative ways for Black to complete his development. However, many King's Indian Defence and Modern Defence themes will feature in the games in this section.

The most obvious way for Black to do this is to capitalise on the fact that - compared with the King's Indian - he has not yet committed himself to ...g6 and ...♗g7 and can therefore try to develop this piece more actively with ...♗c5 or ...♗b4. When White chooses to play a quick e4, his central dark squares can often become a little weak and Black should be looking for opportunities to exploit this. In this context, the more active development of the dark-squared bishop fits the bill well.

As any good King's Indian player will tell you, when the position has been closed with White playing d5, Black should be looking for opportunities to snap away at the white centre with pawn breaks such as ...f5, ...c6 or even ...b5. We see all of these ideas coming into play in the following material.

Game 37
**Farago-Speelman**
*Beersheba 1987*

| 1 | d4 | ♘c6 |
|---|----|----|
| 2 | c4 | e5 |
| 3 | d5 | ♘ce7 |
| 4 | e4 | ♘g6 |
| 5 | ♗e3 | ♗b4+ |
| 6 | ♘d2 | |

6 ♘c3 ♘f6 7 f3 ♗xc3+ 8 bxc3 d6 9 c5 0-0 and Black has a useful lead in development which counter-balances the strength of the white bishop pair.

| 6 | ... | ♘f6 |
|---|-----|-----|

**7　f3**

This creates a dark-square weakness on the g1-a7 diagonal which Speelman rushes to exploit.

**7　...　♕e7!**

Less dynamic, but also perfectly playable for Black is 7...0-0 8 a3 ♗e7 9 ♗d3 d6 10 ♘e2 ♘h5 11 g3 ♗g5 12 ♗f2

♗h3 13 ♘c3 ♘f6 14 ♘f1 ♘e8 15 ♘e3 ♘e7 16 ♕c2 ♗xe3 17 ♗xe3 f5 with a fine game, Iashvili-Z. Nikolic, Belgrade 1992.

**8　♘e2**

Others:

a) 8 ♖c1 led to a complex struggle in Shirazi-Miles, Chicago 1990, viz. 8...c6 9 ♘h3 0-0 10 ♗e2 a5 11 a3 ♗c5 12 ♗xc5 ♕xc5 13 ♘b3 ♕a7 14 d6 a4 15 ♘a1 ♖e8 16 c5 b6 17 0-0 bxc5 18 ♗c4 ♕b6 19 ♖f2 h6 20 ♖d2 ♖a5 21 ♘f2 ♗a6 22 ♗xa6 ♖xa6 23 ♘c2 ♘f4 24 ♘e3 ♘e6 25 ♘c4 ♕b5 26 ♘d3 ♘d4 27 ♖c3 ♘b3 28 ♖f2 ♘d5! 29 exd5 cxd5 and Black went on to win.

b) 8 ♕e2 a5 9 ♕f2 b6 10 ♘e2 ♗c5 11 ♘c1 ♘h5 12 g3 d6 13 ♘d3 ♗xe3 14 ♕xe3 f5 15 exf5 ♗xf5 16 ♘f2 ♘f6 17 ♗d3 ♗xd3 18 ♘xd3 0-0 19 0-0 ♕d7 with an equal position, Collas-Bus, Cappelle la Grande 1992.

For 8 g3 see the game Kaidanov-Miles in the introduction.

**8　...　0-0**

| 9 | g3 |

9 a3 ♗c5 10 ♕b3 a5 11 ♗xc5 ♕xc5 12 ♕c3 a4 13 g3 d6 14 ♘c1 c6 15 ♗e2 ♕a7 16 dxc6 bxc6 17 c5 d5 18 ♘d3 ♗h3 19 ♖g1 ♗e6 20 ♖c1 ♘d7 21 ♘b4 ♖ac8 22 ♔f2 f5 and the insecure position of White's king guarantees Black a good game, Pisulinski-Gdanski, Bydgoszcz 1990.

| 9 | ... | a5 |
| 10 | ♗h3 | ♗c5 |
| 11 | ♕b3 | c6 |
| 12 | 0-0? |

Black has an active position and has certainly vindicated his choice of opening. The incautious text, however, makes matters worse for White. He should first play 12 ♖c1. Now Black breaks his chains on the queen's flank.

| 12 | ... | b5! |

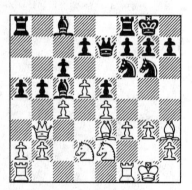

| 13 | cxb5 |

13 dxc6? bxc4 and ...d5 is coming.

| 13 | ... | cxd5 |
| 14 | a4 | d4 |

| 15 | ♗f2 | ♗b4 |
| 16 | ♖ad1 |

16 ♘c4? runs into the tactical trap 16...d5! and Black wins.

| 16 | ... | ♗b7 |

Black has achieved everything he could hope for from the opening. Although White has a protected passed pawn on the queenside Black has a mass of central pawns combined with excellent development. Meanwhile, White's king's fortress is none too solid. The pawn moves in front of White's king represent a permanent weakness in the defensive shield. As soon as Black achieves the key advance ...d5 he will start to punch holes in White's carapace.

| 17 | ♘c4 | d5 |
| 18 | exd5 |

18 ♘b6 is met simply by 18...dxe4! 19 ♘xa8 ♗xa8 20 fxe4 ♘xe4 and Black has overwhelming compensation for the exchange.

| 18 | ... | ♗xd5 |
| 19 | ♕d3 | ♖ad8 |

**20 ♗f5 e4**

A bold and impatient attempt to convert his central advantage into immediate victory by over-running White's king.

**21 fxe4 ♘xe4**
**22 ♘xd4?**

After this White is in terrible difficulties as Black's king's bishop develops ferocious activity. The best chance to defend was 22 ♗xd4 ♘c5 23 ♕c2 ♘b3! and now White cannot afford to lose the dark-squared bishop and so must reconcile himself to 24 ♗f2 ♗xc4 25 ♕xc4 ♘d2 and Black gains the exchange and should win the game easily.

**22 ... ♘xf2**
**23 ♖xf2 ♗c5**

**24 ♕c3?**

Now White loses by force. Others tries are:

a) 24 ♘e3 ♗xd4 25 ♕xd4 ♗b3 winning.

b) 24 ♘xa5 ♗xd4 25 ♕xd4 ♗f3 26 ♘c6 (or 26 ♖xf3 ♖xd4 27 ♖xd4 ♕e1+ and Black wins)

26...♗xc6 27 ♕xd8 ♖xd8 28 ♖xd8+ ♕xd8 29 bxc6 and now Black rounds up the dangerous passed pawn with 29...♘e5 30 ♖c2 ♕b6+ 31 ♔g2 ♘xc6 with an easy win.

c) 24 ♘d2! was the best try, but after 24...♗a8 25 ♘2b3 ♗b6 the black bishops are immensely powerful and White has to deal with the threat of ...♕b7.

**24 ... ♗xc4**
**25 ♕xc4**

25 ♗xg6 hxg6 26 ♕xc4 ♕e5 27 ♖f4 (27 ♖fd2 ♖xd4) 27...g5 28 ♖g4 ♖xd4! 29 ♖gxd4 ♖d8 and wins.

**25 ... ♘e5**
**26 ♕c3 ♕a7!**
**0-1**

The diagonal pin against White's king is deadly, for example, 27 ♖fd2 ♗xd4+ 28 ♖xd4 ♖xd4 29 ♖xd4 ♕xd4+ 30 ♕xd4 ♘f3+ and Black wins on material. A superb vindication of Black's opening against a strong opponent.

Game 38
**Alvarez-Izeta**
*San Sebastian 1993*

| 1 | d4 | ♘c6 |
|---|-----|------|
| 2 | c4 | e5 |
| 3 | d5 | ♘ce7 |
| 4 | e4 | ♘g6 |
| 5 | ♘f3 | |

A natural alternative to this simple developing move is 5 g3, played not so much with the idea of fianchettoing the white king's bishop, but so as to present a discouraging palisade, represented by the white pawn on g3, to the black knight on g6. Nevertheless, this slow treatment does not face Black with any serious problems and he has two ways of continuing, both based on the free development of his king's bishop on c5:

a) 5...♘f6 6 ♗g2 ♗c5 7 ♘e2 h5 8 h3 d6 9 ♘bc3 ♗d7 10 ♕d3 a6 11 a4 h4 12 g4 ♘h7 13 ♗e3 ♕f6 14 ♗xc5 dxc5 15 ♕e3 b6 16 a5 ♘g5 17 axb6 cxb6 18 f3 0-0 and the weak-

nesses in the white kingside give Black a very promising game, Knoll-Mestrovic, Werfen 1993.

b) 5...♗c5 6 h4 h6 7 ♘c3 ♘f6 8 ♗h3 d6 9 ♕f3 c6 10 ♗f5 ♗xf5 11 ♕xf5 cxd5 12 cxd5 0-0 13 ♘ge2 ♘h7 14 ♕f3 ♖c8 15 h5 ♘e7 16 g4 f6 17 ♘g3 ♘g5 18 ♗xg5 fxg5 19 ♘f5 ♘xf5 20 gxf5 ♕b6 21 ♖b1 ♗d4 22 0-0 ♗xc3 23 bxc3 ♕a6 24 ♖fc1 b6 Sitnik-Mestrovic, Portoroz 1996. Black has coped with the white kingside initiative and now stands better thanks to the weak pawns on a2, c3 and e4.

| 5 | ... | ♗c5 |
|---|-----|------|

Move-order is not staggeringly important here. In the game Koemetter-Welling, Velden 1995 Black scored a powerful win with the alternative 5...♘f6 6 ♕c2 ♗c5, viz. 7 ♗e2 0-0 8 0-0 d6 9 a3 a5 10 ♘c3 ♗d7 11 ♘e1 c6 12 ♘d3 ♗d4 (it is surprising how often d4 turns out to be a useful outpost for Black's dark-squared bishop in this variation) 13 ♗g5 h6 14 ♗xf6 ♕xf6 15 b4 ♕g5 16 ♖fc1 f5 (Black is playing in King's Indian style, but with a very powerful king's bishop on d4, instead of its familiar post on g7) 17 ♘e1 ♘f4 18 ♗f1 ♘h3+ 19 ♔h1 ♘xf2+ 20 ♔g1 ♘xe4+ 21 ♔h1 ♘g3+ 22 hxg3 ♕h5 mate.

| 6 | ♗e2 | d6 |
|---|-----|------|
| 7 | 0-0 | a5 |

A useful precaution against possible queenside expansion from White based on a3 and b4. As seems to be the norm in this variation, Black's king's bishop is firmly entrenched on the dark squares and White has no easy way of dislodging it.

| 8 | ♘c3 | ♘f6 |
|---|---|---|
| 9 | ♘e1 | 0-0 |
| 10 | ♘c2 | |

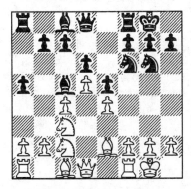

10 ♘d3 is well met by 10...♗d4 when White would already be obliged to resort to the clumsy 11 ♗f3 in order to defend his e4-pawn. The text

prepares the manoeuvre ♗e3, finally challenging the dominance of Black's active bishop.

| 10 | ... | ♗d7 |
|---|---|---|
| 11 | g3 | h6 |
| 12 | ♗e3 | b6 |

Although this renounces any thought of prodding White's centre with ...c6 in the future it is worthwhile gaining play in the soon-to-be-opened b-file if White's insists on trading off Black's bishop.

| 13 | ♗xc5 | bxc5 |
|---|---|---|
| 14 | a4 | |

White moves over to the defence on the queenside, preparing to block the b-file with ♘b5 at some distant date. However, if White instead seeks to keep his options open by means of 14 b3 followed by a3 and b4, Black's counterplay on the other wing with ...♘h7 and ...f5 still gives him the superior chances.

| 14 | ... | ♘h7 |
|---|---|---|
| 15 | ♘e3 | ♘e7 |
| 16 | ♗g4 | f5 |

Achieving his dream advance. Now, after inevitable exchanges on f5 Black will secure all the play in the position, since he is able to press the white camp both on the b-file and the f-file.

| 17 | ♗xf5 | ♗xf5 |
|----|------|------|
| 18 | exf5 | ♘xf5 |
| 19 | ♘xf5 | ♖xf5 |
| 20 | ♕g4 | ♕d7 |
| 21 | h4 | |

To stop ...♘g5.

| 21 | ... | ♖af8 |
|----|-----|------|
| 22 | ♘e4 | |

22 ♘b5 would have been more consistent with his 14th move but White feels that he needs his knight on the kingside for defensive purposes.

| 22 | ... | ♖b8 |
|----|-----|------|

Black immediately exploits the absence of White's knight from its blockading post.

| 23 | ♖ab1 | ♕f7 |
|----|------|------|

White's next move is designed to shore up his queenside and prevent the annoying invasion ...♖b3. Now, though, the

pressure intensifies on the white position from Black's other desirable property, the f-file.

| 24 | b3 | ♖f3 |
|----|-----|------|
| 25 | ♘d2 | ♖d3 |
| 26 | ♖b2 | ♖f8 |

Black's alternating attacks are most attractive. His primary goal has now been achieved: one black rook has penetrated the white position.

| 27 | ♕e2 | ♖d4 |
|----|------|------|
| 28 | ♘e4 | ♕g6 |

| 29 | ♖e1 | ♖f4 |
|----|------|------|

Winning material; the threats of ...♖fxe4 or ...♖xh4 cannot be satisfactorily parried. White's next move is pure desperation.

| 30 | ♘xc5 | dxc5 |
|----|-------|------|
| 31 | ♕xe5 | ♖fe4 |
| 32 | ♖xe4 | ♖xe4 |
| 33 | ♕xc7 | ♖e1+ |
| 34 | ♔g2 | ♕d3 |
| 35 | ♕c8+ | ♘f8 |
| 36 | ♕xc5 | |

Although White, on paper, has more than enough material compensation for his knight, the concentrated power of Black's forces in direct attack against the exposed white king swiftly proved decisive.

| 36 | ... | ♛f1+ |
| 37 | ♔f3 | ♛h1+ |
| 38 | ♔g4 | ♛e4+ |
| 39 | f4 | ♖e3 |

| 40 | ♛c8 | ♛g6+ |
| | 0-1 | |

Game 39
**Stempin-Kuczynski**
*Warsaw 1990*

| 1 | d4 | ♘c6 |
| 2 | c4 | e5 |
| 3 | d5 | ♘ce7 |
| 4 | ♘c3 | ♘g6 |
| 5 | g3 | |

In this variation White tries to restrict the activities of Black's queen's knight on g6 without committing himself immediately to the rigid e4, occupying the centre but at the cost of a general weakening of the dark squares.

| 5 | ... | ♗b4 |

In this situation 5...♗c5 is somewhat less logical. Since White has not played e4 yet, he can always revert at some point to e3, defending the dark squares and blotting out Black's king's bishop. A wild example of this was Lugovoi-Karpachev, Smolensk 1992: 6 ♗g2 a6 7 h4 h6 8 ♘e4 ♗b4+ (after all Black once again resorts to placing his bishop on b4) 9 ♔f1 f5 10 a3 ♗f8 11 h5 ♘6e7 12 d6 ♘c6 13 dxc7 ♛xc7 14 ♘c3 ♘f6 15 ♘f3 d6 16 ♘h4 ♘e7 17 ♘d5 ♘fxd5 18 cxd5 ♗d7 with an unclear position.

| 6 | ♛b3 | |

This is the type of formation where White would prefer to avoid doubled pawns. The text seeks to achieve this whilst simultaneously gaining a tempo against the black bishop. Against 6 ♛c2 Black has two methods of proceeding, either the restraint of White's queenside pawns, combined with the retention of Black's king's bishop or an acquiescence in the exchange of bishop for knight, with the expectation that Black will in return gain a lead in development and prospects of harassing the white queen. Here is one example of each:

a) 6...a5 7 a3 ♗e7 8 h4 d6 9 e4 h6 10 ♗h3 ♗xh3 11 ♘xh3 ♘f6 12 ♗e3 ♘f8 13 0-0-0 ♘8d7 14 f3 ♘c5 15 ♘f2 ♘fd7 16 ♔b1 ♘b6 17 ♘d3 ♘xd3 18 ♕xd3 ♘d7 19 ♘b5 ♖a6 20 ♖h2 a4 21 ♕f1 0-0 22 ♕h3 c6 and Black's queenside play keeps the game in a state of dynamic equality, Barlov-Z. Nikolic, Yugoslav Ch. 1985.

b) 6...♘f6 7 a3 ♗xc3+ 8 ♕xc3 0-0 9 h4 ♘e4 10 ♕c2 f5 11 ♗g2 d6 12 ♘h3 h6 13 h5 ♘e7 14 ♗xe4 fxe4 15 ♕xe4 ♗f5 16 ♕g2 ♗g4 17 f3 ♗xh5 18 ♘g5 ♗f7 19 ♕h3 ♕c8 20 e4 ♕xh3 21 ♘xh3 ♗h5 22 g4 ♗e8 23 ♔f2 b5 and Black has a slight initiative, Agrest-Miles, Münster 1993.

| 6 | ... | ♕e7 |
|---|-----|-----|
| 7 | a3 | ♗a5 |
| 8 | ♕c2 | ♗b6 |

To meet the threat of b4 and c5 by White, Black could also play 8...♗xc3+ 9 ♕xc3 ♘f6 reaching something similar to Agrest-Miles, quoted above.

| 9 | h4 | d6 |
|---|-----|-----|
| 10 | ♘a4 | |

White speculates on the variation 10...♘f6 11 h5 ♘f8 12 h6 g6 13 ♗g5 with a powerful pin, but Black's next move preempts this.

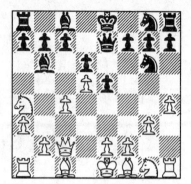

| 10 | ... | h6 |
|----|---------|-------|
| 11 | ♘xb6 | axb6 |
| 12 | e4 | ♘f6 |
| 13 | ♗d2 | ♗d7 |
| 14 | h5 | ♘f8 |
| 15 | f3 | ♘8h7 |

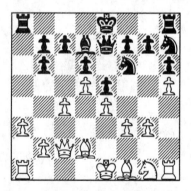

Strategically, Black faces difficulties in that White can blockade the kingside with g4 whilst possessing the long-term advantages of the bishop pair and mobile queenside pawns. Tactically, though, Black is in fine shape since White's ambitious and time-consuming manoeuvres on both flanks have deprived his king of any permanently secure shelter. White's kingside is full of holes whilst, on the queenside, Black controls the only open line (the a-file) and can add further fuel to the flames with breaks such as ...c6 and ...c5.

| 16 | ♘e2 | 0-0 |
|----|-----|-----|
| 17 | ♘c3 | ♘e8 |
| 18 | 0-0-0 | |

There is a strong case here for sealing things up with g4. White takes a gamble by allowing Black to counter with ...f5. After 18 g4 ♕f6 19 ♗e2 ♘g5 20 ♕d3 c6 21 0-0-0 ♘c7 22 ♔b1, for example, White has the plan of ♖df1 and f4 with all to play for. Indeed, the whole notion of a concerted attack against f3 by means of ...♕f6 may be too ambitious. Hence, White could certainly count on equality by playing g4. After the text, a hand-to-hand fight ensues.

| 18 | ... | ♘g5 |
|----|-----|-----|
| 19 | ♗g2 | f5 |

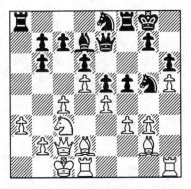

| 20 | f4 |
|----|-----|

White loses patience and allows Black everything he is hoping for. He was doubtless concerned that against slower means Black would trade on e4 and follow up with moves like ...♗g4 and ...♘f6, fixing the White pawn on h5 as an irrevocable weakness for the endgame.

| 20 | ... | ♘xe4 |
|----|-----|------|
| 21 | ♘xe4 | fxe4 |
| 22 | ♗xe4 | ♘f6 |

| 23 | ♖de1 |
|----|------|

Giving in without a fight and ceding Black global control of all the crucial light squares. White should at least have tried 23 ♗g6 when matters are not yet clear.

| 23 | ... | ♘xe4 |
|----|-----|------|
| 24 | ♕xe4 | ♗f5 |
| 25 | ♕e2 | ♕d7 |

Black does not need to defend what remains of his pawn centre. The light-square counterattack initiated by this move will prove more than adequate compensation for any slight material loss.

equally fatal.

| | | |
|---|---|---|
| 26 | fxe5 | ♕a4 |

| | | |
|---|---|---|
| 29 | ♔d2 | ♕c2+ |
| 30 | ♔e3 | |

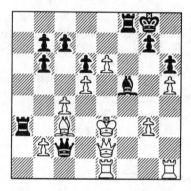

| | | |
|---|---|---|
| 27 | ♗c3 | ♕b3 |
| 28 | e6 | |

| | | |
|---|---|---|
| 30 | ... | ♖xc3+ |

**0-1**

He may as well try to cement his ill-gotten gains in as much as the defensive 28 ♔d2 allows 28...♖xa3 29 bxa3 ♕c2+ 30 ♔e3 ♕xc3+ with a winning attack. In this line the humbly palliative 29 ♕d1 fails just as dismally to 29...♕xc4 30 bxa3 ♕d3+ 31 ♔c1 ♕xc3+.

### Game 40
### Komarov-Zagema
*Dortmund 1992*

| | | |
|---|---|---|
| 1 | d4 | ♞c6 |
| 2 | c4 | e5 |
| 3 | d5 | |

| | | |
|---|---|---|
| 28 | ... | ♖xa3 |

This irruption is again

Compared with the Budapest Gambit capturing on e5 is not worrying. Let us first examine what happens in the cognate gambit line: 1 d4 ♞f6 2 c4 e5 3 dxe5 ♞g4 4 ♞f3 ♗c5 5 e3 ♞c6 6 ♞c3 and now Black can recapture his gambit pawn with 6...♞gxe5. In comparison after 3 dxe5 in the main game Black does not have to waste tempi in order to recapture his pawn. Here is one example 3 dxe5 ♞xe5 4 e3 ♞f6 5 ♞f3 ♞xf3+ 6 ♕xf3 d5 7 h3 ♗e6 8 ♞c3 ♗b4 (Black already has an active position) 9 ♗d2 0-0 10 0-0-0 dxc4 11 e4 ♘d7 12 ♘d5 ♗xd2+ 13 ♖xd2 c6 14 ♕f4 cxd5 15 exd5 c3 16 bxc3 ♕a5 17 dxe6 ♕xc3+ 18 ♔b1 fxe6 19 ♕d4 ♕xd4 20 ♖xd4 ♘b6 21 f3 ♖ad8 22 ♖d3 ♘d5 23 a3 ♖d6 24 g3 ♖b6+ 25 ♔a2 ♖c8 26 ♖b3 ♖c2+ 27 ♔b1 ♖xb3+ 28 ♔xc2 ♖xa3 29 ♗e2 ♖a2+ 30 ♔d3 b5 0-1 Trivuncevic-Mestrovic, Ljubljana 1994.

**3 ... ♘ce7**

An interesting alternative is for Black to develop his king's bishop before retreating the knight. Play then has some similarities to that typical of the Bogo-Indian (1 d4 ♘f6 2 c4 e6 3 ♘f3 ♗b4+), e.g. 3...♗b4+ 4 ♘d2 ♘ce7 5 a3 ♗xd2+ and now:

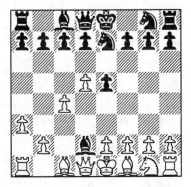

a) 6 ♗xd2 d6 7 g3 (7 e4 ♘g6 8 ♕c2 f5 9 exf5 ♘h4 10 g3 ♘xf5 11 ♘e2 ♘f6 12 ♗g2 0-0 13 0-0 ♕e8 14 ♖ae1 ♕h5 15 ♕c3 ♘h6 16 f3 ♘f7 17 ♕e3 ♗d7 with an easy game for Black, Semkov-Rossi, Forli

1988) 7...♘f6 8 ♗g2 0-0 9 ♘f3 a5 10 b4 ♘e4 11 0-0 ♘xd2 12 ♕xd2 b6 13 ♖ac1 axb4 14 axb4 ♗g4 15 ♘e1 ♖a4 16 ♘c2 ♕d7 17 c5 bxc5 18 bxc5 ♕b5 and Black has successfully freed his position, Koch-Becker, Bundesliga 1992.

b) 6 ♕xd2 d6 7 ♕g5 (this strange queen sortie hopes to force a weakness with ...g6, but Black proves that he does not have to be so accommodating) 7...h6 8 ♕xg7 ♘g6 9 ♘f3 ♘f6 10 ♘g5 ♕e7 (after 10...hxg5 11 ♗xg5 White regains the piece, but the simple text move leaves the white queen stuck) 11 g4 (this is necessary as Black was threatening ...♘h5, snaring the white queen) 11...♘xg4 12 ♘e4 ♗f5 13 ♘g3 ♗d7 14 ♗h3 0-0-0 15 ♗xg4 ♗xg4 16 ♘e4 ♗f5 17 ♘f6 ♘f4 18 e4 ♗g6 19 ♖g1 ♘h5 20 ♘xh5 ♗xh5 21 ♕g3 and the complications have resulted in equality, Justo-German, Buenos Aires 1995.

**4 ♘c3**

The pseudo-pin with 4 ♗g5 does not seem to serve any particularly useful purpose, e.g. 4...h6 5 ♗h4 c6 6 e4 ♕a5+ 7 ♕d2 ♕xd2+ 8 ♘xd2 ♘g6 9 ♗g3 ♘f6 10 ♘gf3 ♗b4 11 a3 ♗xd2+ 12 ♘xd2 c5 13 f3 d6 14 ♗f2 b6 15 ♘b1 ♗d7 16 ♘c3 ♔e7 17 ♔d2 ♘e8 18 h4 h5 19 ♗e3 f5 20 ♗d3 f4 21 ♗f2 ♘c7 and the black knights are more useful than the white bishops in this blocked position, Thaler-

Summerbauer, Austria 1993.

**4  ...  d6**

Hitherto we have examined variations where Black has played 4...♘g6 with the plan of liberating his king's bishop either on c5 or b4. The text is an alternative in which Black allows himself the possibility of an immediate rupture of the centre based on ...f5. However, we must caution that this places a great deal more stress on Black's structure than the fluid piece development lines arising from 4...♘g6.

**5  e4**

**5  ...  f5**

5...g6 6 ♗d3 f5 7 exf5 ♘xf5 8 ♘f3 ♗h6 (this exchange is positionally desirable but Black must now play with care as he has fallen behind in development) 9 ♗xh6 ♘gxh6 10 ♕d2 ♘f7 11 0-0-0 ♘h4 12 ♘xh4 ♕xh4 13 g3 ♕h6 14 f4 ♗g4 15 ♖df1 0-0-0 and Black has safely co-ordinated his forces and can look to the future with confi-

dence, Stojnic-Soln, Bled 1996.

**6  ♗d3**

An alternative is 6 ♘f3 ♘f6 7 ♗d3 and now 7...f4 or even the adventurous move 7...h6 perhaps planning ...g5.

**6  ...  ♘f6**

**7  ♗g5**

7 ♘f3 would transpose to the previous note. The text hopes for 7...fxe4 8 ♘xe4 ♘xe4 9 ♗xe4 when Black is virtually paralysed.

**7  ...  f4**

Black does not oblige and switches instead to an advance which is, as we have already seen, typical for Black's counterplay in this line.

**8  g3**

White essays a head-on assault and the game soon develops along the uncharted and tactically rich contours which all black players who employ this variation should desire. The more rigidly positional course is 8 ♗xf6 gxf6 9 ♕h5+ ♘g6 10 ♗e2 ♕d7 11 h3 with the plan of ♗g4 to control the light squares. This is, perhaps, the way Karpov would have proceeded and White's grip on the light squares gives him the advantage.

**8  ...  ♘g6**

**9  h4**

In contrast to the basically strategic treatment outlined above, White's bull-in-a-china-shop approach here gives Black time to consolidate.

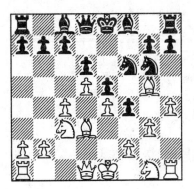

| 9  | ...  | fxg3 |
| 10 | fxg3 | ♝e7  |
| 11 | h5   | ♞f8  |

In view of the threat of ...♞xd5, neatly bagging a pawn, White must now retreat.

| 12 | ♝e3 | ♞g4 |
| 13 | ♝d2 | ♞f6 |
| 14 | ♞f3 |     |

Of course 14 ♝e3 would lead to repetition.

| 14 | ... | ♞8d7 |
| 15 | b4  |      |

Depriving Black of the c5-square for his knight.

| 15 | ... | a5 |

| 16 | a3  | 0-0 |
| 17 | ♝e2 | ♞b8 |

Black's queen's knight, after a wondrous series of gyrations, finally reaches home. Indeed, Black's entire game plan appears to be based on the systematic undevelopment of his pieces but, in the mean time, there have been compensations. By rushing his pawns forward on both flanks, White has exposed himself to severe counter-punches.

| 18 | ♞h4  | axb4 |
| 19 | axb4 | ♖xa1 |
| 20 | ♛xa1 | ♞a6  |
| 21 | ♛b1  |      |

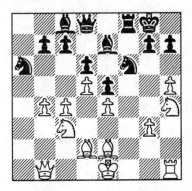

| 21 | ... | c6 |

Black's counterplay takes on definite shape. What had once looked like a significant space advantage for White now resembles more a position shot through with gaps and weaknesses.

| 22 | dxc6 | bxc6 |
| 23 | b5   |      |

For his troubles White does

at least create an instant passed pawn, though one that can be fairly easily blockaded.

| 23 | ... | cxb5 |
|----|-----|------|
| 24 | cxb5 | ♘c5 |
| 25 | ♗c4+ | |

Black cannot now evade this check with 25...♔h8 on account of 26 ♘g6+ hxg6 27 hxg6+ with an immediate win for White.

| 25 | ... | ♗e6 |
|----|-----|------|
| 26 | ♗xe6+ | ♘xe6 |

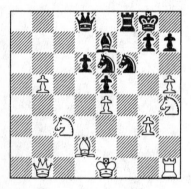

**27 ♘f5**

It is worth considering here 27 ♕a2 to slow down Black's occupation of the centre.

| 27 | ... | ♘d4 |
|----|-----|------|
| 28 | ♘xd4 | exd4 |
| 29 | ♘e2 | d5 |

With White's forces scattered around the perimeters, his king stuck in the centre, and with Black now possessing a passed pawn of his own, it is evident that White's entire strategy has collapsed.

| 30 | ♘xd4 | ♕b6 |
|----|-----|------|
| 31 | ♕a1 | ♗c5 |

This would also have been the answer to 31 ♘c6.

| 32 | ♗e3 | ♗b4+ |
|----|-----|------|
| 33 | ♔d1 | |

33 ♗d2 ♗xd2+ 34 ♔xd2 ♘xe4+ is hopeless.

**33 ... ♕c5**

If immediately 33...♘xe4, 34 ♕a6 keeps White afloat. However, 33 ♘g4 looks quite decisive.

**34 ♕a6**

If 34 ♕c1 ♗c3 35 ♘e2 d4, 36 ♕xc3! but 34...♕e7 still leaves White with the insuperable task of holding his passive legions together.

| 34 | ... | ♕c4 |
|----|-----|------|
| 35 | ♘f5 | ♕d3+ |
| 36 | ♔c1 | ♗a3+ |
| | **0-1** | |

A scrappy game in which the advantage swung to and fro. Its chief merit lies in its demonstration of the resilience of Black's position. Even though White appeared to be driving Black back on all fronts Black's position remained sound and was quite capable of delivering a decisive counter-punch when White's pawn structure became bloated and unwieldy after his early and ruthless attempt to gain space on all fronts.

### Game 41
**Juraczka-Palos**
*Oberwart 1991*

| 1 | **d4** | **♘c6** |
|---|--------|---------|
| 2 | **c4** | **e5** |
| 3 | **♘f3** | |

This transposes to a version of the English Opening in which Black has a comparatively easy time.

| 3 | ... | **e4** |
|---|-----|--------|
| 4 | **♘g5** | |

An alternative is 4 ♘fd2, but Black can still gain excellent counterplay, e.g. 4...f5 5 e3 ♘f6 6 ♘c3 ♗b4 7 ♗e2 0-0 8 0-0 ♗xc3 9 bxc3 d6 10 ♗a3 ♖e8 11 c5 d5 12 ♖b1 ♘e7 13 c4 c6 14 ♕c1 ♕c7 15 cxd5 cxd5. Here Black can consolidate his queenside most effectively by means of the manoeuvre ...♗d7-c6 and meanwhile he is ready to advance powerfully on the other flank. Sugden-Keene, Cambridge 1969 continued 16 f4 exf3 17 ♘xf3 ♘g6 18 ♗b5 ♗d7 19 ♕c3 ♗c6 20 ♗c1 ♖e7 21 ♗d3 ♘e4 22 ♗xe4 fxe4 23 ♘g5 ♕d7 24 ♖b2 ♗b5 25 ♖ff2 ♗c4 26 ♕c2 ♕g4 27 ♘h3 ♖f8 28 ♖xf8+ ♘xf8 29 c6 bxc6 30 ♖b8 (at long last White, with his threat of ♗a3, appears to have gained palpable counterplay but unfortunately for him Black is ready with a swift tactical refutation) 30...♖f7 31 ♘f2 ♖xf2 32 ♔xf2 ♕h4+ 0-1.

White's problem in this game was the inflexibility of his central and queenside pawns. Nevertheless, if White seeks to preserve his pawns intact with 7 ♕c2 0-0 8 a3 ♗xc3 9 ♕xc3 then Black can still gain his fair share of the centre with 9...d5 10 b3 ♘e7 followed by ...c6 and ...♗e6 is quite satisfactory for Black. The long-term aim is to strike at White's kingside with ...f4 and the closed nature of the position renders White's advantage of the two bishops somewhat nugatory.

| 4 | ... | **♗b4+** |
|---|-----|----------|
| 5 | **♘c3** | |

Any other move would lose the knight on g5, but as it is now Black can smash White's pawns.

| 5 | ... | **♘f6** |
|---|-----|---------|

**6   e3**

6 d5 is more combative than the text, but Black is still able to gain good play by wrecking White's pawn structure, e.g. 6...♗xc3+ 7 bxc3 ♘b8 8 g3 d6 9 ♗g2 ♕e7 10 c5 ♗f5 11 cxd6 cxd6 (White has managed to dissolve the doubled c-pawns, but the weakness on the c-file remains) 12 0-0 h6 13 ♘h3 0-0 14 ♗e3 ♘bd7 15 ♕d2 ♘e5 with a good game, van den Donk-Lemmers, Netherlands 1994.

It is also worth pointing out a trap that has claimed many victims. After 6 ♕b3? Black can in fact snatch the white pawn on d4 with 6...♘xd4 since 7 ♕xb4 is foiled by 7...♘c2+, snaring White's queen.

| 6 | ... | ♗xc3+ |
|---|-----|-------|
| 7 | bxc3 | d6 |
| 8 | h4 | h6 |
| 9 | ♘h3 | g5 |

An ingenious move, utilising the potential pin on the h-file to lock White's knight out of play.

| 10 | ♘g1 | g4 |
|----|-----|-----|
| 11 | ♘e2 | ♘h5 |

Maintaining the theme of dominating White's knight.

| 12 | g3 | f5 |
|----|-----|-----|
| 13 | ♘f4 | |

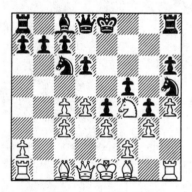

At last White's knight emerges, but the resultant positions is inimical to White's bishops. Black now proceeds to besiege White's weak pawn on c4.

| 13 | ... | ♘xf4 |
|----|-----|------|
| 14 | exf4 | b6 |
| 15 | ♗e3 | ♘a5 |
| 16 | ♗e2 | ♗a6 |

| 17 | ♖b1 | c5 |
|----|-----|-----|
| 18 | 0-0 | ♕d7 |

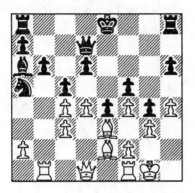

Black has to neutralise White's possibility of ♕a4 before annexing the c4 pawn. Black now has a classic won position, with a blockade that robs White of any possibility of active counterplay.

| 19 | ♖b5 | ♗xb5 |
|----|-----|-------|
| 20 | cxb5 | c4 |
| 21 | d5 | ♕xb5 |
| 22 | ♕d4 | 0-0 |

| 23 | h5 | ♖ac8 |
|----|-----|-------|
| 24 | ♗xg4 | fxg4 |
| 25 | ♕xe4 | ♕e8 |
| 26 | ♕h1 | ♕e7 |
| 27 | f5 | ♔h7 |

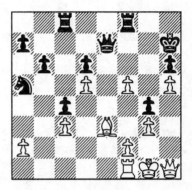

| 28 | f3 | 0-1 |
|----|-----|-----|

The final blunder since Black can now play ...♕xe3+. It is notable that when thrown on their own resources and unable to follow established theory, so many white players succumb so quickly.

# 6   1...♘c6 against Flank Openings

In this chapter we consider the viability of opening 1...♘c6 against moves other than 1 d4 or 1 e4.

The main point of the interpretation of ...♘c6 that we suggest in this book is to angle for a quick ...e5. Therefore, although 1...♘c6 is perfectly playable against 1 c4, Black then does best to continue with a quick ...e5 transposing to lines of the English. An in-depth analysis of these variations is beyond the scope of this book, but in this chapter we suggest methods for Black to combat White's various options.

The encounter chosen for our stem game is an old one, but it is one that has been overlooked in many anthologies and excellently demonstrates many of the themes of this particular variation.

### Game 42
**Capablanca-Bogoljubow**
*Nottingham 1936*

#### 1   c4

In this particular game White diverts play into lines of a strict English Opening with the fi-anchetto of the white king's bishop exerting pressure against Black's queen's flank.

In the following analysis we consider 1...♘c6 against other White openings:

a) 1 b3 was popularised by Larsen in the late sixties and early seventies. However, ceding the centre so early to Black is not to everyone's taste. Black can meet this move comfortably with 1...♘c6 2 ♗b2 e5, e.g. 3 e3 d6 4 ♗b5 (against other continuations, Black can successfully adopt a King's Indian formation where the white bishop on b2 plays a minimal role in proceedings, e.g. 4 ♘e2 g6 5 d4 ♗g7 6 d5 ♘ce7 7 ♕d2 ♘f6 8 c4 0-0 9 ♘bc3 c6 10 g3 cxd5 11 cxd5 ♗d7 and Black has the initiative, Minasian-Wolff, Glendale 1994; or 4 c4 g6 5 g3 ♗g7 6 ♗g2 h5 7 h3 h4 8 g4 f5 9 ♘c3 ♘f6 10 gxf5 ♗xf5 11 d3 g5 and Black has very good play, Bagirov-Gelfand, Amsterdam 1989) 4...♗d7 5 ♘e2 a6 6 ♗xc6 ♗xc6 7 0-0 ♕g5! (an excellent move which drives White into a passive position as 8 ♘g3 h5 9 f4 ♕g6, threatening ...h4 is very unpleasant) 8 f3 ♘f6 9 c4 d5

10 ♘bc3 (Adams suggests that White's best is 10 f4! exf4 11 ♘xf4 dxc4 12 bxc4 ♗d6 13 ♗xf6 ♛xf6 14 ♘c3 which is unclear) 10...0-0-0 and Black has a good game, Minasian-Adams, Debrecen 1992.

b) 1 f4 ♘c6 is perfectly playable. If White now heads for a king pawn opening with 2 e4, Black should change plan and play 2...d5 and if 3 e5 then 3...♗f5 with an improved version of Nimzowitsch's original treatment.

Better for White is 1 f4 ♘c6 2 ♘f3 when Black can play 2...d5 (also possible is 2...d6, intending ...e5), e.g. 3 g3 (3 e3 ♗g4 4 ♗b5 e6 5 0-0 ♘ge7 6 b3 d4 7 e4 a6 8 ♗d3 ♘b4 and Black stands well, Parr-de Coverly, Hastings 1995) 3...♗g4 4 ♗g2 ♛d7 5 ♘c3 0-0-0 6 h3 ♗xf3 7 ♗xf3 ♘f6 8 d4 ♘e4 with active play, Tu Hoang Thong-Kagan, Melbourne 1994.

c) 1 ♘f3 is often an indica-tion that White wants to play an English Opening, but without allowing Black the option of the ...e5 variations. Against such a player, 1...♘c6 is a good reply. Now (after 1 ♘f3 ♘c6) 2 c4 e5 or 2 g3 e5, Black gets the varia-tions which White may be try-ing to avoid. If White changes tack with 2 e4 d6 or 2 d4 d5 then Black has again obliged White to enter channels with which he may be unfamiliar.

d) 1 g3 ♘c6 is obviously per-fectly playable for Black and is likely to transpose into lines of the English Opening.

e) 1 ♘c3 is often used as a transpositional device. For ex-ample 1 ♘c3 d5 2 e4 and now 2...d4 and 2...dxe4 have inde-pendent significance, but 2...e6 and 2...c6 transpose respectively into the French Defence and Caro-Kann Defence.

However, our key defence still holds good. 1 ♘c3 ♘c6 and now 2 e4 can be met by 2...e6 3 d4 ♗b4.

Furthermore, after 2 d4 e6 White really has nothing better than 3 e4 ♗b4 with the same position.

An interesting example of play from this position is: 4 ♘f3 (4 a3 ♗xc3+ 5 bxc3 d6 6 ♕g4 ♕f6 7 ♕g3 ♕g6 8 ♕xg6 hxg6 9 f4 b6 10 ♘f3 ♗b7 11 ♗d3 ♘a5 12 0-0 c5 with a solid position for Black and chances to play against White's weakened pawn structure, Angqvist-Hjelm, Stockholm 1992) 4...d6 5 ♗d2 (5 ♗b5 a6 6 ♗e2 ♘ge7 7 ♕d3 0-0 8 a3 ♗a5 9 0-0 e5 10 d5 ♘b8 11 ♘d2 ♘d7 12 b4 ♗b6 13 ♗g4 ♗d4 14 ♘b3 ♗a7 15 ♘a4 ♕e8 16 ♘c3 f5 and Black has active play as in Stertenbrink-Dausch, Bundesliga 1984) 5...♘ge7 6 a3 ♗a5 7 ♗d3 0-0 8 0-0 ♘g6 9 h3 ♗b6 10 ♘e2 (10 d5 exd5 11 exd5 ♘ce5 is pleasant for Black) 10...♘h4 11 ♘xh4 ♕xh4 12 ♗e3 e5 13 c3 f5! 14 exf5 ♗xf5 15 ♗xf5 ♖xf5 16 ♕d2 (better is 16 dxe5 ♖xe5 17 ♗xb6 axb6 maintaining an equal position) 16...exd4 17 cxd4 ♖af8 18 ♖ad1 ♔h8 19 ♖fe1 h6 20 f3 d5 21 ♗f2 ♕d8 22 ♘c1 ♕f6 23 ♖e2 ♖g5 24 ♔h1 ♕g6 25 ♗g1 ♕h5 26 ♕e1

*(see following diagram)*

26...♖xf3! (the tactical culmination of Miles's patient manoeuvring) 27 ♖e8+ (27 gxf3 ♕xh3+ 28 ♖h2 ♕xf3+ 29 ♖g2 ♕xg2 is mate, while 27 ♖f2 ♘xd4! 28 gxf3 ♘xf3 29 ♕e6

♗xf2 30 ♗xf2 ♘e5 is also hopeless for White) 27...♔h7 28 ♕e6 ♖xh3+ 0-1 David-Miles, Linares Z 1995.

f) 1 b4!? is the only move we feel a slight reluctance to recommend 1...♘c6 against. We leave it to readers to decide if 2 b5 ♘e5 3 ♗b2 ♘c4!?

(or, perhaps more cautiously, 3...♘g6) gives Black a playable position.

| 1 | ... | ♘c6 |
| 2 | ♘c3 | e5 |

Having staked his claim in the centre, Black will now aim

to gain space on the kingside with ...f5 which can also act as a prelude to a potential kingside attack.

We have now entered the realms of the English Opening. The following notes and variations are not intended to be definitive, but to suggest sensible choices for Black against the various possible schemes of development by his opponent.

**3 g3**

After 3 ♘f3 a good line for Black is 3...f5, e.g. 4 d4 e4 and now:

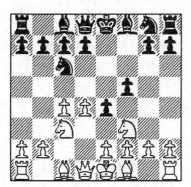

a) 5 ♘g5 ♗b4 6 ♘h3 ♘f6 7 e3 ♗xc3+ 8 bxc3 d6 9 ♗e2 0-0 10 0-0 ♕e7 11 f3 ♗d7 12 fxe4 ♘xe4 13 ♕c2 ♖f6 with a promising kingside initiative, Ubilava-Kurajica, Las Palmas 1994.

b) 5 ♗g5 ♗e7 6 ♗xe7 ♘cxe7 7 ♘d2 (7 ♘g1 ♘f6 8 e3 d6 9 h4 c6 10 ♘h3 ♗e6 11 ♗e2 ♗f7 12 ♘g5 0-0 13 ♕b3 ♕b6 with a good game for Black, Vaganian-Pr. Nikolic, Barcelo-

na 1989) 7...♘f6 8 e3 0-0 9 ♗e2 d6 10 0-0 c5 11 ♘b3 b6 and Black again stands well, Gulko-A.V. Ivanov, USA Ch. 1989.

**3 ... g6**
**4 ♗g2 ♗g7**
**5 d3**

An alternative here for White is 5 e3 when Black can try to gain space on the kingside with 5...f5 and now:

a) 6 d4 e4 7 ♘ge2 ♗g7 8 ♘f4 ♘e7 9 h4 d5 10 b3 c6 11 ♗a3 ♗h6 12 ♗f1 ♗xf4 13 gxf4 ♗e6 14 ♕d2 ♔f7 with an equal game, Korchnoi-Salov, Wijk aan Zee 1992.

b) 6 ♘ge2 ♘f6 7 0-0 0-0 8 d3 ♘e7 9 e4 d6 10 exf5 ♘xf5 11 ♘e4 ♘xe4 12 ♗xe4 c6 13 ♕b3 ♖f7 14 f4 exf4 15 ♗xf4 ♗e6 and Black has no problems, Sher-Hodgson, Isle of Man 1995.

**5 ... d6 (D)**
**6 ♗d2**

The main point of this move is to defend White's queen's

knight against possible Black
tactics based on ...f5 and ...e4.
Once the knight is defended,
White can launch a quick strike
on the queenside by means of
♖b1 and b4.

After 6 ♘f3 Black can again
aim for his usual kingside expansion with 6...f5, e.g. 7 ♖b1
a5 8 a3 ♘f6 9 0-0 0-0 10 b4
axb4 11 axb4 h6 12 b5 ♘e7 13
♗b2 ♗e6 14 ♖a1 ♖c8 (14...♖b8
15 c5 ♘d7 16 ♘a4 dxc5 17 ♖a3
g5 18 ♕a1 ♘g6 19 ♘d2 ♕e7
20 ♘c3 ♘f6 21 ♖a7 b6 22 ♕a6
♖fd8 23 ♖d1 ♕f7 24 ♖b7 ♖xb7
25 ♕xb7 ♘e8 26 ♘c4 e4 27
♘e3 f4 0-1 Urban-Soffer, Budapest 1993) 15 c5 ♘d7 16
cxd6 cxd6 17 ♘a4 d5 18 ♘d2
♕e8 with a complex game, Iv-
anchuk-Topalov, Wijk aan Zee
1996.

| 6 | ... | f5 |
|---|---|---|
| 7 | ♖b1 | ♘f6 |
| 8 | b4 | 0-0 |
| 9 | b5 | ♘e7 |

Here Alekhine recommended
9...♘d4 10 e3 ♘e6.

| 10 | ♕c2 | h6 |
|---|---|---|

The long range intention is to
march forwards on the king's
flank with ...g5 and ...f4.

| 11 | e3 | a6 |
|---|---|---|

An interesting decision which
was criticised at the time. It
seems that the queenside is
White's domain and it is folly
by Black to provoke a skirmish
there. The point, though, is to
disturb White's planned onrush
of pawns on the queenside by
gaining counterplay on the open
a-file.

| 12 | a4 | |
|---|---|---|

Here 12 bxa6 ♖xa6 13 ♗xb7
♗xb7 14 ♖xb7 ♕a8 exposes
White's rooks to all sorts of
unpleasant tactics. That would
also be the reply if White were
to capture on b7 over the coming moves.

| 12 | ... | c5 |
|---|---|---|
| 13 | bxa6 | ♖xa6 |

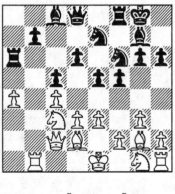

| 14 | ♘ge2 | ♘c6 |
|---|---|---|
| 15 | ♘d5 | ♘xd5 |
| 16 | ♗xd5+ | ♔h7 |
| 17 | h4 | |

Capablanca liked this kind of manoeuvre which both inhibits ...g5 and prepares long term pressure against Black's kingside.

| 17 | ... | ♕e8 |
| 18 | ♔f1 |

White's idea is to plant his king on g2 where it would stay in perfect safety, but Bogoljubow's clever play never gives Capablanca time to carry out this manoeuvre. In view of that the uncomplicated 18 ♗g2 is stronger to be followed by ♖b5 and a5 when White retains some pressure against Black's b7-pawn.

| 18 | ... | ♘e7 |

After this there is no way that White can avoid the exchange of his strong bishop.

| 19 | a5 | ♘xd5 |
| 20 | cxd5 | ♕f7 |
| 21 | ♕c4 | f4! |

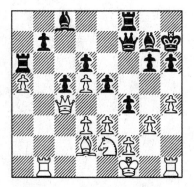

Without this White would slowly consolidate and eventually break into Black's position via the b-file. The long range

strategy for White would be ♔g2 followed by doubling rooks on the b-file and then ♖b6. Just in time, though, Bogoljubow activates the inherent dynamism of his position and launches a power counter-attack along the light squares.

| 22 | gxf4 | ♗g4 |
| 23 | ♖g1 | ♗f3 |
| 24 | e4 | exf4 |
| 25 | ♘xf4 |

Although this looks extremely promising the pawn capture under-estimates Black's chances. Alekhine recommended instead 25 ♕b5.

| 25 | ... | ♗e5 |
| 26 | ♘e6 |

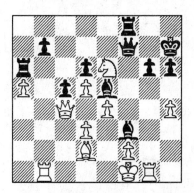

This seems crushing and it is hardly surprising that Capablanca could not resist playing it. It should be noted on the other hand that 26 ♘xg6 ♖g8 27 h5 fails to 27...♗h2.

| 26 | ... | ♖aa8 |

Black cannot move his rook from f8 since, for example, 26...♖e8 fails to the tactic 27

♗xh6 ♚xh6 28 ♕c1+.

| 27 | ♘xf8+ | ♖xf8 |
|----|-------|------|
| 28 | ♕b5 | |

In his haste to exchange queens Capablanca overlooks a defensive resource. 28 ♗e3 ♗h2 29 ♖g2 ♗xg2+ 30 ♚xg2 ♗e5 31 ♚f1 ♕d7 would be correct when Black has compensation for his pawn, but nothing more.

| 28 | ... | ♗xe4! |
|----|-----|-------|

Capablanca had probably only expected 28...♗e2+ 29 ♚xe2 ♕xf2+ 30 ♚d1 ♕xg1+ 31 ♚c2 when White's king has escaped immediate danger and the b7-pawn falls after which White has a dangerous passed a-pawn.

| 29 | ♕xb7 | |

Suddenly Capablanca has to fight for a draw.

| 29 | ... | ♗xd3+ |
|----|------|-------|
| 30 | ♚g2 | ♗e4+ |
| 31 | f3 | |

The saving grace which deflects Black's bishop. If instead 31 ♚h3 then 31...♗f5+ follow-ed by ...♗d7 evading the queen exchange and leaving White's king hopelessly exposed.

| 31 | ... | ♗xf3+ |
|----|------|-------|
| 32 | ♚h3 | ♗xd5 |
| 33 | ♕xf7+ | ♖xf7 |
| 34 | ♖gf1 | ♗e6+ |

Now Black has all the chances but White can ultimately save himself with ♗f4, trading off one of Black's dangerous bishops.

| 35 | ♚g2 | ♗f5 |
|----|------|------|
| 36 | a6 | ♗e4+ |
| 37 | ♚h3 | ♖g7 |
| 38 | ♖b6 | ♗f5+ |
| 39 | ♚g2 | ♗e4+ |
| 40 | ♚h3 | ♖e7 |

Also inadequate for a win is 40...g5 41 hxg5 hxg5 42 ♚g4.

| 41 | ♗f4 | ♖f7 |

| 42 | ♗xe5 | |

The final liquidation which ensures a draw.

| 42 | ... | ♖xf1 |
|----|------|------|
| 43 | ♗xd6 | ♖f3+ |
| 44 | ♚h2 | g5 |
| 45 | hxg5 | hxg5 |
| 46 | ♗xc5 | ½-½ |